Stranger
DANGER
How to
Keep Your
Child Safe

Stranger
DANGER
How to Keep Your Child Safe

CAROL SORET COPE

 CADER BOOKS · NEW YORK

ANDREWS AND MCMEEL
A UNIVERSAL PRESS SYNDICATE COMPANY
KANSAS CITY

Thank you for buying this Cader Book—we hope you enjoy it.
And thanks as well to the store that sold you this, and the hardworking
sales rep who sold it to them. It takes a lot of people to make a book.
Here are some of the people who were instrumental:

Editorial: Bradford Telford, Verity Liljedahl, Jake Morrissey, Dorothy O'Brien,
Regan Brown, Nora Donaghy
Design: Charles Kreloff
Copy Editing/Proofing: Bill Bryan
Production: Carol Coe, Traci Bertz, Cathy Kirkland
Legal: Renee Schwartz, Esq.

Printed in the United States of America

If you would like to share any thoughts about this book, or are interested in other
books by us, please write to: Cader Books, 38 E. 29 Street, New York, NY 10016.

Or visit our web site: http://www.caderbooks.com

Library of Congress Cataloging-in-Publication Data
Cope, Carol Soret
    Stranger danger : how to keep your child safe / Carol Soret Cope.
  — 1st ed.
      p. cm.
    "Cader books".
    ISBN 0-8362-2758-1 (pbk.)
      1. Child sexual abuse—United States—Prevention. 2. Abduction—
United States—Prevention. 3. Children and strangers—United States.
4. Child sexual abuse—Prevention—Study and teaching—United States.
5. Abduction—Prevention—Study and teaching—United States. I. Title.
HV6570.2.C66   1997
613.6—dc21   96-53644
                                                                  CIP

March 1997

First Edition

10 9 8 7 6 5 4 3 2 1

Attention Schools and Businesses: Andrews and McMeel books are available for
educational, business, or sales promotional use. For information, please write to:
Special Sales Department, Andrews and McMeel, 4520 Main Street,
Kansas City, Missouri 64111.

CONTENTS

A PERSONAL NOTE TO PARENTS

This is a book I never wanted to write. Like most of us, I avoided the subject of child abuse, especially child sexual abuse and molestation. Even though I am a parent, and a former school psychologist, I didn't think this was anything I needed to know about. It couldn't happen to my child. It couldn't happen here.

Fortunately, it didn't happen to my child, but I now understand that this was largely luck and circumstance rather than anything special I did to protect her.

But it did happen here, practically in my backyard, in Homestead, Florida. In September 1995, nine-year-old Jimmy Ryce was abducted as he walked home from his school bus stop, a distance of only five blocks. Three months later, the man who allegedly molested and murdered him led police to the child's remains. I didn't know Jimmy or his parents, Claudine and Don Ryce. But this was too close to home.

I had been researching a novel, and as part of that work I viewed a videotaped polygraph examination of a Boy Scout leader accused of molesting three young boys in his troop. Robert Rios, the polygraph examiner, told me that the man had passed the test. Rios and I watched the videotape together, and in the postexamination interview, under Rios's expert questioning, the man eventually admitted that he had actually molested *twenty-seven* young boys in his troop.

As I drove home, I thought, Thank God my child is grown now! I knew then that I would have to write this book.

Law enforcement and child treatment experts warn that there is a virtual epidemic of child sexual abuse sweeping our country. In unprecedented numbers, estimated at nearly half a million per year, our children are targets of sexual assault, sometimes violent. No one has a clear explanation for this alarming development. But whatever the cause, parents must recognize that their children may be at risk.

There is an area of child sexual abuse that this book does not address: intrafamilial abuse. Experts say that in most child molestation cases, the molester is a family member; and child abduction is most often committed by a noncustodial parent seeking to regain "possession" of a child after divorce. The dynamics of these intrafamily crimes require separate consideration, which is beyond the scope of this book.

This is a book for parents to use in addressing the most important part of their job: keeping their children safe. Experts say that child protection is harder now than ever, but this doesn't mean that you and your child are helpless. There is much you can do to protect your child, and to help safeguard all our children. This book will show you how to do that.

ACKNOWLEDGMENTS

So many talented, committed people gave generously of their time and effort to make this book possible. They have my deepest appreciation.

First, I'd like to thank all the law enforcement professionals. At the U.S. Customs Service in Miami, Special Agent in Charge Bonni Tischler; Assistant Special Agent in Charge Keith Prager; Public Information Officer Michael Sheehan; and Special Agents Rachel Cannon, Catherine Sanz, Aida Perez, Gary Narz, Mike McCage, Kathryn Dellane, and Lindsay LaJoie all spent countless hours with me, for which I'm very grateful. Sergeant David Robshaw of the Broward County Sheriff's Office was also very helpful, and I thank him. And to my friend Robert Rios, an excellent polygraph examiner, my thanks for sharing his expertise with me, and wrangling permission for me to attend a fascinating conference. I have the highest regard for all these talented, committed people, and I'm deeply grateful for their help.

At the U.S. Attorney's Office in Miami, Assistant U.S. Attorneys Marilyn Butler and Guy Lewis generously shared their insight and experiences with me, for which they have my appreciation.

Psychologists contributed invaluable assistance to this project. My gratitude goes especially to the remarkable Dr. Marilyn Segal at Nova University in Fort Lauderdale, Florida, for her expert guidance with this project. Thanks also to Dr. David Finkelhor at the University of New Hampshire, and Dr. Dennison Reed, Plantation, Florida, for their assistance and advice. And my personal gratitude to Dr. Philip Boswell and Dr. Elizabeth Gilmore for their encouragement and support.

I am especially grateful to Nancy McBride, the powerhouse director of the Florida Branch of the National Center for Missing and Exploited Children, and to John Sullivan, former special agent in charge of the U.S. Customs office in West Palm Beach, Florida, now director of the Graduate Program in Criminal Justice at Lynn University in Boca Raton, Florida. Between them, Nancy and John know everything worth knowing about this subject—or they know who does. They steered me in the right direction so many times, and they have my deepest gratitude.

Teresa Klingensmith, Esq., the manager of Legislative Affairs at the NCMEC, was extremely helpful with the legal and legislative aspects of this project. Thanks to Kenneth Lanning of the FBI, who took the time to share his thoughts with me.

My thanks also to Craig Stein, friend and colleague, who was, as always, supportive, smart, and kind. And my deepest appreciation to Don and Claudine Ryce, whose courage and compassion are an inspiration to all of us. Our sympathy and our hearts are with you always.

Last but not least, thanks once more to my tireless agent, John Boswell, for his expertise, his vision, and his commitment to this challenging project.

Working with all of you has brought back a sense of balance. Yes, there are people who do bad things to children. But there are also people like you who spend their lives doing good for children they don't even know. It has been a privilege.

Stranger
DANGER
How to Keep Your Child Safe

PALS AND STRANGERS: RECOGNIZING A CHILD MOLESTER

A twenty-eight-year-old drifter who lives in a van on the beach. The neighborhood handyman, a reliable worker who keeps to himself. A well-known minister in a fundamentalist church. A popular Boy Scout leader. A husband and wife who operate a day care center for preschoolers. The high school band teacher. A respected counselor who administers programs for abused children. A forty-two-year-old male attorney, married, with a young stepdaughter. A successful, middle-aged corporate executive. A multimillionaire entrepreneur.

What do these people have in common? They're all child molesters.

It's difficult to find reliable statistics on the number of children who are sexually molested in this country each year. Experts say that people are reluctant to report these crimes to police, and that only one-third to one-half of actual crimes are reported. In 1994, *reported* instances of child sexual abuse totaled 431,000. Using these figures, experts calculate that the number of children sexually assaulted by someone other than a family member was 30,000 to 50,000. And this is a conservative number. Assuming that only half of such crimes are reported, the actual number of children who are targets of sexual abuse by a non–family member could approach 100,000 annually in this country.

Whatever the actual number may be, law enforcement and child treatment experts agree on one thing: The number of sex crimes aimed at children is increasing dramatically. The American Medical Association recently warned, "Sexual assault is a silent, violent epidemic growing at an alarming rate and traumatizing the [women and] children of our nation." Dr. Jon Shaw, director of child and adolescent psychiatry at the University of Miami's School of Medicine, sees a vicious circle: Nearly 70 percent of adolescent sex offenders report that they themselves were sexually abused as children.

Experts also say that when a child is sexually molested, chances are about two out of three that the molester is someone the child knows rather than a stranger. For parents, this means that keeping your child safe entails much more than simply warning him about strangers.

Mental health professionals and law enforcement experts use various terms to describe and define different kinds of sexual offenders who prey upon children. For our purposes, any adult who engages in sexual activity with a child is a child molester. As the above examples demonstrate, anyone can be a child molester. This problem cuts across racial, cultural, socioeconomic, and educational lines, and includes both men and women. However, the overwhelming majority of convicted child molesters are male; therefore this book uses masculine pronouns to refer to molesters. Masculine pronouns are also used to refer to children, to simplify the text, and also to remind parents of an important fact: Boys may be just as much at risk for molestation as girls. Any child can become the victim of a child molester.

According to psychologists, some of these sexual predators are opportunists who will attack any vulnerable victim they can find—a child, an elderly person living alone, or a handicapped person, for example. Others are adults whose sexual orientation is exclusively toward children, usually children of a particular age range and gender. These distinctions help alert parents to the dangers posed by two general types of child molesters that are important for us to consider: the "pal" and the "stranger."

The child molester masquerading as a pal is someone the child knows and probably likes: a favorite teacher or coach, for example, the boy scout leader or church youth group leader, even a relative. The pal molester has some social and intellectual skills, and, most important, he has well-developed, often sophisticated techniques for obtaining his victims. He is the insidious, seductive molester who "understands" kids and gets along well with them; he's often described as "just like a big kid himself." His home may be filled with video games, toys, sports equipment, electronic equipment, and movies that his target-age children like. Sometimes he creates a virtual playground to appeal to his victims, complete with amusement rides and pets. The pal arranges special activities for kids— picnics, games, parties, sleepovers, camping trips. These events usually exclude other adults, especially parents.

By contrast, the stranger is an adult who is not a regular part of the child's life. He appears, either by chance or by design, wherever the child is. He's the man who stops his car near the sidewalk and asks your child for directions. He's the friendly man in the park, or the nice guy at the next video game in the arcade. He may use coercion, force, manipulation, or a lure to snare a victim. Specific examples of the techniques used by child molesters will be discussed in the third chapter (page 29), along with strategies to help your child avoid becoming the victim of a stranger molester.

Once the stranger molester has obtained a victim, he may sexually assault the child and then let him go. But sometimes, especially if he fears capture or if he is a sexual sadist, the molester will murder the child. According to Kenneth Wooden, an expert in this field, the life expectancy of a child abducted by such a molester is fourteen to forty-eight *hours.*

These stranger abduction/murders are relatively rare—estimated by some experts at 300 to 400 cases annually. But although this number seems low, many more children are actually targets of unsuccessful abductions. Statistics collected by the U.S. Department of Justice indicate that in 1990 there were 114,600 attempted abductions of children by non–family members. And when these crimes are completed, they are the most horrifying tragedies in the headlines: Polly Klaas in Petaluma, California, for example, and Jimmy Ryce in Homestead, Florida. For these child victims, there is no therapy or treatment. There is no second chance at life.

In terms of sheer numbers, experts say that a child is more likely to be victimized by a pal-type child molester: an adult the child knows. Parents need to understand that the pal molester intentionally places himself in a position of access to children, and of respect or authority with adults—especially the parents of his victims. He is often described as "above suspicion," a pillar of the community, "a saint." A pal.

Here's one recent example. Three young boys told their parents that their Boy Scout leader had molested them. The parents notified police. When word of the accusations got out, other parents of Boy Scouts were shocked and disbelieving. The scout leader was a nice guy, friendly and helpful to parents, popular with his scouts. He couldn't do such a thing. Could he? The leader vehemently denied any improper conduct and agreed to take a videotaped polygraph test. He passed the test—and then, under skillful questioning by an expert polygraph examiner, he confessed to molesting *twenty-seven* young scouts in his troop over a two-year period. Even worse, he had also permitted an adult buddy to molest these boys along with him. And this wasn't the scout leader's first offense.

Law enforcement authorities were not shocked by the scope of his offense. According to experts, such a molester may begin to molest by age fifteen; and once he starts to have sexual contact with children, he becomes a voracious predator who is always on the prowl for child victims. Some experts estimate that such a molester may victimize 300 children before he's caught the first time, and that during his "career," he is likely to have up to 500 child victims. Others give more conservative estimates, suggesting that the "average" number of victims for a child molester is around 235. Whatever the actual number may be, the experts agree on one thing: With this type of serial child molester, finding and obtaining victims becomes the driving force in his life.

This molester has a voracious sexual appetite for children. This is partly inclination and partly simple arithmetic. Remember that the child molester usually has a preferred age for his victims. Since children are always growing up, this molester's victims inevitably mature out of the preferred age range fairly quickly. When that happens, he has to replace them. He has to locate and obtain new child victims who are the "right age." This is a never-ending process that consumes nearly all his time, energy, and attention. Just as the rest of us get up and go to work each day, the serial child molester uses every day to hunt for more victims. The only time he will not be on the prowl for children is when he's in jail. According to authorities, this is the reason such child molesters dread jail time: It's the one place where there's absolutely no chance of access to child victims. As soon as they're back on the street, these molesters immediately resume sexual stalking of children.

These molesters often keep collections of "trophies" or "souvenirs" from their child victims: a baseball cap, clothing, sports equipment, a favorite toy or game. They often take photographs of their victims, through either persuasion or subterfuge. Some of the pictures are sexually explicit, while others chronicle the child's development much like school photos. Such molesters often create and maintain elaborate photograph albums of their victims as if the molester and the child were lovers—which, in the molester's mind, they are.

For example, Florida police recently arrested a child molester and seized an unusual collection of photographs from his home. According to authorities, this man was known and trusted by the parents of his victims, who were all young boys. He invited potential victims for outings on his power boat, invitations that never included parents or other adults, but since the man seemed so "nice," the boys were permitted to go. He would take the boat out and anchor it, then he and his young male guests would dive and swim in the ocean. On these outings, the man showed the boys his underwater camera and told them that he was trying it out while they were swimming. In reality, he was taking close-up photographs of the boys' crotches as they swam and played together. He developed these photographs himself, making enlargements, creating a montage of images. For this molester, it was the first step in initiating sexual contact with his victims.

A more virulent manifestation of the molester's impulse is hardcore child pornography: visual depictions of children engaged in explicit sexual conduct with other children, with adults, even with animals. Child molesters often maintain extensive collections of child pornography in pictures and videotapes, and some of it is particularly vicious, ugly, sadistic, and violent. These collections are very important to the molester as objects for fantasizing, for trading with other molesters, and, as discussed in the third chapter (page 29), for use with child victims in breaking down their inhibitions about sexual conduct, or blackmailing them into keeping the "secret" of the molester's activities. Child pornography is evidence that a crime has been committed, and it is an instrumentality of crime, not "just dirty pictures" like adult pornography or obscenity. Child pornography is also a trail that may lead to someone who is fantasizing about sexual conduct with children but hasn't yet made contact with live victims.

Law enforcement experts and psychologists recognize the crucial role that child pornography plays for these child molesters. In the past, child pornography was difficult to obtain. Because it was often imported from foreign countries and sold through the mail, the U.S. Postal Inspector and U.S. Customs Service joined forces to intercept child pornography and prosecute those who bought or sold it by mail. Now, however, electronic technology has changed the rules—to the molester's advantage. A virtual smorgasbord of child pornography and child molester "support groups" is available on the information superhighway. The "adult" bulletin boards available via a home computer allow these molesters to gather on-line and swap child pornography in voluminous amounts, with astonishing speed, and in complete anonymity. Worse, they describe for each other their fantasies of sex with children, thus "validating" their own desires and encouraging each other to act on their fantasies. The logical next step is to go on-line trying to set up live meetings with real kids. Or they look for prey closer to home, in our neighborhoods and schools.

Medical experts fear that increased computer contact among such molesters could undo years of treatment for "recovering" child molesters or people with latent emotional problems in this area. "You are putting incredible temptation in front of people who already have incredible frustrations themselves," says Fred Berlin, founder of the Johns Hopkins Sexual Disorders Clinic. "Suddenly, a world of temptation opens up that wasn't there before."

Douglas Rehman, an undercover "cybercop" for the Florida Department of Law Enforcement, described three recent cases in which the arrested molester never attempted any contact with young children before going on-line. According to Rehman, cybercops aren't making progress against the avalanche of child molesters on-line. "It's worse, much worse than when we started," Rehman says.

Some of these child molester groups are informal, but others are highly structured, efficient organizations. The best known among law enforcement officials are the Rene Guyon Society, the Lewis Carroll Collector's Guild, and the North American Man-Boy Love Association (NAMBLA). NAMBLA professes to believe that children have a right to "sexual freedom," that is, to have sexual contact with adults. This organization advocates weakening the legal protection of children from sexual predators by such means as lowering the age for consent to sexual relations. Of course, no responsible person takes this rhetoric seriously. NAMBLA is engaged in thinly disguised efforts to legitimize the sexual molestation of children by adults. But the organization is very active. It puts out a newsletter espousing its "philosophy" and advising members on methods of seducing children. There's no doubt among professionals that this type of conduct provides aid, comfort, and encouragement to such molesters.

What makes someone act this way? What is the cause of such voracious sexual deviancy? No one knows exactly how or why a person becomes a child molester, what "makes" someone act this way. But experts agree on this: There is no known "cure." According to Dr.

Parker Elliott Dietz, a professor of law and psychiatry at the University of Virginia and renowned expert in this field, the problem is that most serial child molesters don't want to change, to be "cured," even after they've been arrested and incarcerated. Nor is the threat of another arrest enough to deter them. No matter how much remorse they may express, how many promises they make, once they're out of jail, their first priority is to find more child victims. As Dr. Dietz testified at the sentencing hearing of a convicted child molester, "What we have no treatment for is the aspect of character or personality that leads a person to repeatedly act on such a preference."

Some experts focus their efforts on treatment, rehabilitation, and containment for child molesters rather than a "cure." However, there is little agreement among the experts on what constitutes effective treatment, and which offenders are good candidates for rehabilitation. Under these circumstances, containment of the molester and prevention programs seem to be the community's best hope of protecting its children.

How can parents identify a molester in their child's world? There's no single reliable test, but there is a constellation of characteristics to watch for. The serial child molester is most likely a single male, over twenty-five, who lives alone or with parents or other relatives. He probably doesn't date. If he is or has been married, it is probably to a strong, domineering woman or a weak, passive woman-child. In either case, he has a "special" relationship with his spouse that involves little sexual contact.

The pal molester establishes regular access to children and displays excessive interest in them. He relates better to kids than to other adults and has a circle of "friends" who are young. He's the one who's always arranging outings for kids, offering to baby-sit, suggesting sleepovers. First, he seduces parents with his interest in their child and his apparent recognition of how "special" the child is. A single mother, in particular, may believe that this nice guy is just the "male influence" her child needs. In reality, he's the worst possible "friend" for a child. Then the pal molester seduces the child victim with attention, affection, and gifts. He's always there, always ready to listen, always available. If your child's adult "pal" seems too good to be true, he probably is.

As alarming as these molesters are, remember that you and your child are not helpless victims. Now that you know something about the characteristics of the pal molester and the stranger molester, there are steps you can take to keep these predators out of your child's world. The following are general suggestions, and they do not cover every situation. Use this list as a guide to help you develop a plan of action for your child's world.

1. Make sure that people in regular contact with your child—schoolteachers, scout leaders, church group leaders, day care workers, volunteers, etc.—are properly screened and evaluated. Don't just assume that the organization has "taken care of it." Meet with your school principal, the school board, the minister, the rabbi, etc., and request a copy of the organization's policy and procedure for screening employees *and volunteers* who work with children. Then be sure that the procedure has been followed.

2. When you hire someone to spend time with your child—a babysitter, housekeeper, tutor, coach—ask for references and then check them out. Get a social security number and driver's license number. Then call your local police department and ask them to find out whether the individual has a criminal record. Many states have laws requiring that a list of the names and addresses of convicted child molesters be maintained. Your local police department can tell you whether there is such a list in your state and, if so, how to find out whether someone you want to employ is on the list.

3. Minimize the opportunity for the stranger's chance access to your child. As much as possible, make sure your child is not alone in public. Even in their own neighborhoods, young children should be accompanied by a parent or trusted adult. Older children, including teenagers, should travel in groups. Remember that the stranger looks for a vulnerable victim—a child alone in a situation where the molester is not likely to be seen or stopped.

4. Organize your neighbors to be observant for strangers in your neighborhood. If there's a suspicious car or person on your street,

notify each other and call the police. Be sure to provide as much information as possible: a description of the car, tag number, description of the driver, etc.

Remember, your goal as a parent is prudence, not paranoia. You want to do everything you can to keep your child safe, to be sure that your child, like most kids, grows up healthy and happy.

WHO IS MOST VULNERABLE?

John Sullivan has devoted his professional life to tracking and apprehending child molesters. Until his retirement in 1996, Sullivan was the special agent in charge of the West Palm Beach, Florida, office of the U.S. Customs Service, where he developed and implemented a program to combat the transmission of child pornography by computer. He is now the director of the Graduate School of Criminal Justice at Lynn University in Boca Raton, Florida.

For the past several years, Sullivan has worked closely with Nancy McBride, director of the Florida Branch of the National Center for Missing and Exploited Children, in developing and presenting a child safety seminar for parents and professionals.

A renowned expert in this field, Sullivan often begins a training session with parents like this:

Close your eyes and relax, he tells the parents. Get comfortable. Now, recall the most idyllic day of your own childhood. Where were you that day? Remember the sights, the sounds, the smells. How old were you then? How did you feel that day? Maybe the sun was warming your body as you floated in a pool or on a lake. You were completely relaxed, just enjoying being a kid. You felt safe, happy, loved. Remember the feeling? Just floating along. Life was good. Remember?

(Now he throws a heavy book to the floor. At the resounding crash, the parents jump, startled, confused. They look around the room, at him, at each other.)

You've just been sexually molested, he tells them. For you, childhood is over.

According to experts, the child molester devours the innocence and emotional health of his victims. The child who has been sexually molested is robbed of some of the basic psychological components of childhood: trust in adults, sense of self-worth, and feelings of security and safety. Psychologists who work with these child victims report symptoms of depression, loss of self-esteem, feelings of guilt, fear, nightmares, sadness, social isolation. Even when there is no physical injury, the psychological trauma can linger for years. With emotional support and therapy, children can overcome these devastating effects. But even under the best circumstances, John Sullivan says, there is no "cure" for the child victims of sexual molestation.

From the molester's viewpoint, children are ideal prey. *Every* child is a potential victim simply because he is a child: physically smaller and less powerful than the adult who stalks him, and less sophisticated. Younger children, especially, are easily manipulated by adults. Naturally curious about the world, they are interested, trusting, open to new experiences. All these normal attributes of childhood make them vulnerable.

Although it may be comforting to think that child abduction happens only in the city or only in "bad" neighborhoods, experts say this isn't true. *Any* child—especially a child alone—is a target for forcible abduction by a predator. These children fit no particular profile except presenting opportunity, however fleeting, to the abductor. In a recent, highly publicized tragedy in Florida, nine-year-old Jimmy Ryce disappeared while walking home from his school bus stop, a distance of only five blocks. Jimmy lived in Homestead, twenty-five miles south of Miami, a bucolic area of farms and horse ranches, where many residents had moved to escape big-city crime. After three months of frantic searching, Jimmy's parents learned that their son had been abducted by a stranger—allegedly by a handyman who had been working nearby. Police believe that he had been cruising the neighborhood in his truck that afternoon, looking for a child to abduct. When he saw Jimmy walking alone, he pulled a handgun and forced the child into the truck. After sodomizing Jimmy, the molester allegedly used the gun to murder him. Eventually he led police to the child's dismembered remains.

Jimmy's father, Miami attorney Don Ryce, reminds us that it's not just the child victims and their families who suffer. "These crimes tear the very fabric of our society," he says. "They diminish our whole social order."

Tragically, Jimmy Ryce was simply in the wrong place at the wrong time. He was a random target of opportunity in this stranger abduction. It can happen anywhere. And it can happen to any child.

By contrast, some children are more vulnerable than others to molesters who use seduction rather than force to obtain their victims. These molesters, usually "pals," are often very skilled not only at employing effective techniques to ensnare children, but also at identifying the children who will be the most vulnerable to their advances. Like a lion that selects a single animal from a herd of prey, these child predators quickly identify their best targets and then move in.

Law enforcement specialists know these dynamics. A federal undercover agent in the field recently remarked, "Give me a day in a fifth grade classroom and I'll pick out the kids most likely to be victimized by a child molester."

Who are the most vulnerable children? In general, they are the neediest kids. The "loner," the social outcast, or the child who simply doesn't have many friends. The child who doesn't get much attention or supervision at home, who craves adult attention, affection, and approval. Or the child who is under some unusual stress, possibly because of problems at home, however mild or temporary. Even well-adjusted, normal children and teenagers go through periods of stress, tension, and insecurity. Especially during adolescence, they may seek to test parental limits and authority, become more independent and adventurous, even rebellious. To the child molester, these are opportunities to be exploited.

Experts recommend that parents be aware of and responsive to their child's moods and emotions. We know that all children have periods of moodiness, but if a child seems fearful, withdrawn, or unhappy for weeks or months, professional assistance may be helpful. In choosing someone to work with a child, experts suggest that a parent get recommendations from someone they trust—a teacher, counselor, pediatrician, minister, or rabbi. Professional credentials and references should be checked.

Unwittingly, and with the very best intentions, parents often play right into the hands of the child molester. With very young children, parents may encourage or even insist that the child be physically affectionate with another adult, regardless of the child's own feelings. Give Aunt Jane a hug, they say. Kiss Uncle Ernie good night. Taken to an extreme, children may learn to "be nice" to adults by touching, kissing, hugging, even when they don't really want to. They see that this pleases their parents. This pleases the adults. With this groundwork already laid by the child's own parents, the pal molester can more easily seduce the child into physical contact under the guise of affection, overcoming any hesitancy the child may feel. After all, this is how the child has learned to "be nice" to adults.

Experts recommend that parents teach their child how to distinguish a "good" touch from a "bad" touch, or a confusing touch. A good touch is a truly affectionate touch. A pat on the back from a friend, a hug from a parent, any touch that makes the child feel happy. A bad touch is an uncomfortable touch, one that hurts or makes the child apprehensive or unhappy. That kind of touch can be almost anything: excessive tickling, hugging, or kissing that doesn't stop when the child wants to stop; or a rough touch, pinch, or slap.

Some touches may be confusing to a child or make him worry, even though they are not painful. An example is a touch on a private area of the child's body, even if it seems accidental or feels momentarily pleasurable. Experts recommend that whenever an adult touches a child in a way that feels bad or is confusing to him, the child should tell the person to stop touching him. Then he should leave and tell a parent about it.

Parents teach older children to be polite to grown-ups, not to embarrass adults or make them "feel bad." We want our children to be helpful, to respect authority and obey adults—opening the door for an adult, for example, or carrying packages to the car, giving directions to a "lost" adult, doing little chores or favors when an adult asks, especially if that adult appears disabled. Yet these are the very traits a clever molester will use against his intended victim. The notorious Ted Bundy, convicted of the savage rape-murders of young women, often used a fake cast on his arm to persuade his victims to "help" him put schoolbooks in his car. Several young women paid with their lives for their generous impulse to be helpful to this expert predator.

Many parents believe that older children and teenagers are less likely targets for strangers because they are more knowledgeable and sophisticated than young children. Experts in child sexual abuse and abduction disagree. Indeed, some authorities say that children aged eleven to seventeen are actually the *most* vulnerable to stranger abduction. A personable, attractive stranger with a good line still gets results with this age group, as Ted Bundy proved, over and over again.

Another way parents inadvertently make their children more vulnerable to seduction by a child molester is by failing to provide age-appropriate sex education. We know that even young children are naturally curious about sex. As they mature, they become much more interested in sex and they develop an active sex drive. If sex is a taboo subject between parent and child, the child will acquire information (or misinformation) from other sources: friends, kids at school, movies, magazines, etc. This situation is ideal for the pal molester. He is ready and willing to exploit the child's natural interest in sex and his lack of access to accurate information. The molester's goal is constant: to entice or seduce the child into sexual activity.

Many parents assume that girls are more vulnerable to molestation than boys. Consequently, they may be more protective of their daughters and permit their sons more freedom, less scrutiny and supervision. Our culture sees boys as more adventurous and assertive than girls, and there's a tendency to believe that they can take care of themselves. But boys may also be less cautious about possible danger, and they may be more reluctant to report molestation, especially if it has occurred while the boy was disobeying parental rules. In fact, experts tell us that boys are about as likely to be victimized as girls. Parents must recognize that their sons may be as vulnerable as their daughters. Remember, the goal is safety for all children, regardless of age or gender.

Now that you know more about the child as victim, there are steps you can take to minimize your child's "victim" characteristics. Use the following guidelines to help you.

1. Experts recommend that young children not be encouraged to kiss or hug an adult if they are reluctant. Physical affection should be entirely spontaneous on the child's part, they say.

2. If your child expresses dislike or discomfort around an adult, accept his feelings. Don't try to convince your child that he doesn't "really" feel that way, or that the adult would be hurt.

3. Let your child know that he can talk to you about *anything*, and that you'll always listen.

4. Consider age-appropriate sex education for your child. Many parents are uncomfortable discussing this topic with their children, but experts say it's important.

5. Stay in touch with the adults who see your child: teachers, scout leaders, counselors, coaches, church leaders. Tell them that you're an interested parent, and request that they call you immediately if they have any concerns about your child.

Remember: Anything that increases your child's self-esteem and his bond with you will make him less vulnerable to a molester.

WHAT MOLESTERS DO AND HOW THEY WORK

Many parents have heard the puppy story: At the park, a friendly stranger appears with a picture of a puppy in one hand and an empty leash in the other. He approaches a young child playing alone. Have you seen my puppy? he asks. Here's his picture. His name is Charlie and he's lost. Will you help me find him? The child is last seen walking off with the stranger (with a horrified parent looking on from a park bench!), calling, Charlie! Charlie!

You may have seen this on television. This incident has been recreated on *Oprah* and elsewhere by Kenneth Wooden, a former teacher and journalist. Wooden has developed a program called "Child Lures" to educate parents and children about the most common lures used by child molesters, and how to avoid them. In his television demonstrations, Wooden used young children and parents who were certain they'd taught their children to say no to strangers. In every instance, the child left with the stranger—on average, within *thirty five seconds.*

The parents who watched their children in these demonstrations were shocked and upset to the point of tears. They'd been sure their children wouldn't even *talk* to a stranger, let alone walk off into the bushes with the man. After a similar event staged by another professional, the children were interviewed and asked this question: Are you supposed to talk to strangers? No, most replied. Then why did you talk to the man with the puppy picture? Why did you go with him? Because "he wasn't a stranger," an articulate little girl explained to the interviewer. "He was a nice man."

To children, a stranger is a bogeyman, a monster, not an attractive, friendly, "nice" man. So our warning "Don't talk to strangers" doesn't really protect them in these situations. In the next chapter, we'll address the issue of how to explain to children that they must not talk to these people, whether they seem to the child to be "strangers" or "nice" people.

A more recent if no less sinister example of stranger abduction occurred in a Florida mall video arcade. An adult player struck up a conversation with a young boy playing at the next video game. The boy seemed to be alone. After a few preliminaries the stranger said, I have a video game I bought for my son, but I'm not sure he'll like it. Would you take a look and tell me if it's the kind you'd like to have? It's outside in my car. The boy left the mall with the man.

Here's the dilemma: As parents, we teach our children to respect and obey adults, especially authority figures such as teachers and police officers. We know that our child's life may someday depend upon following an adult's directions in an emergency, like a fire, for example, or an accident. We also teach them to be helpful and polite to adults—not to intentionally make anyone "feel bad." Yet these good intentions play right into the hands of strangers who stalk our children. In both examples above, the children responded to an adult stranger's request for assistance. They were merely trying to be helpful to a "nice" man.

Many of the stranger abductor's ploys are already familiar to parents. The stranger may use a weapon, as happened with the abduction of Jimmy Ryce at gunpoint in Florida. He may use the threat of force or actual force, especially with a young child. In one common scenario, the stranger stops his car beside the curb and asks a child for directions; trying to be helpful, the child approaches the car and is pulled inside. Or the stranger may simply manipulate a child into a situation where he and the child are alone. For example, a man wearing a phony uniform or badge approaches a child, calls the child by name and says, Your mother's been hurt in an accident. I'll take you to the hospital. Or he knocks on the door when the child is home alone and persuades the child to let him in.

Some of the predator's techniques are versions of offering "gifts" to children, calling to mind the old warning: Don't take candy from strangers. Especially with younger children, the predator may use items such as a toy or game to get the child alone. With older children, some predators are even more blatant—offering attractive, expensive items such as sports equipment or video equipment, or even money, in exchange for sex.

In one recent incident in a Southern state, a friendly man was living in a motor home near a popular beach. He always seemed to be hanging around young boys, Rollerblading with them, playing Frisbee or volleyball on the beach, swimming and body surfing. He provided sports equipment to boys who didn't have any. He bought snacks for the boys and invited them into his motor home to watch videos and read magazines. He told these boys they could choose any "gift" they wanted from the selection he kept in his motor home: a toy or video game, a movie, a pair of skates.

Although the molester's initial approach was disguised as friendliness, he quickly made his intentions known to his targets. Two young boys found a policeman nearby and complained that this "friendly" man tried to solicit them for sex in exchange for these "gifts." Police arrested the man and impounded his motor home. Inside they found a virtual department store inventory of items chosen to appeal to young boys: box after box of brand-name athletic shoes in various colors, styles, and sizes; Rollerblades and other expensive sports equipment; designer jeans and pricey athletic clothes; the latest video games and hand-held Game Boys, and current action/adventure movies; and, inevitably, an extensive collection of erotic and pornographic pictures, magazines, and videotapes—including child pornography.

The two young boys who reported the predator had not, in fact, been molested by him. They resisted his aggressive, overt advances, became frightened, and found the police. But many other young boys in the area had been victimized by the clever, relentless seduction of this voracious predator.

Parents should let their child know that he is not to accept gifts without their permission. Remind young children that gifts are exchanged among friends and families on special occasions such as birthdays and religious holidays. Of course, gifts can be given at other times, for no special reason. But older children should be told that a molester could try to use a "gift" as a bribe to gain access to a child victim, or to bribe the child into silence. Teach your child that he should not accept a gift from an adult, especially anything expensive, without your consent. This means all adults except relatives and those you have designated as trusted adults. Parents should be aware of their child's clothes and belongings, and not hesitate to ask where he got some new, expensive item.

Your child may express fear that he'll lose a friend if he follows the rules outlined here. Reassure him that real friends understand these rules, and they won't stop being your friend. This is the time to reinforce communication with your child, letting him know that he can tell you about anything that's bothering him.

As the child predator knows, it's just a question of finding out what the target-age child will respond to and then playing it out. Remember that these predators know and understand kids, especially kids in their target age range. They're skilled at discovering what these kids like, want, and will respond to.

With older children, the promise of drugs or alcohol may work, or an invitation to an "adult" party. For this reason, experts recommend drug and alcohol education for adolescents and teenagers. Many schools, community agencies, and police departments provide such programs. Find out what's offered in your area and decide whether to include this in your child's education.

Even the offer of a job can be a powerful tactic. This might be a "spontaneous" offer from someone who asks your child to carry something into the house for him in exchange for a few dollars. It could be an advertisement for a job that doesn't exist, or it could be a bona fide job that the molester then uses to establish and maintain contact with a victim. Older kids are usually eager to earn some extra money, and predators exploit this situation. Experts suggest that even adolescents and teenagers should not accept a job without their parents' permission. They recommend that, where appropriate, a parent accompany the child to the job interview. If this is not possible, parents should talk with the child's prospective employer by phone. Get references for the employer, then check them out.

Taking advantage of changing times and technology, these predators are constantly trying out new techniques that parents may not be aware of. Especially where older children and teenagers are targeted, these techniques may be quite sophisticated. A common one is a new version of the old "I'm going to make you a star" routine. On a recent television exposé, for example, teenage girls at a mall were approached by a phony "talent scout" who told them they were being considered to appear on MTV. The girls were thrilled—MTV! After a few minutes of flattery, the "talent scout" asked them to accompany him to "an audition"—an almost irresistible prospect. All the girls left the mall with the stranger.

If your child is interested in beginning a career in modeling, acting, or sports, he must, of course, discuss this with you. If you decide to support your child's ambitions, contact a legitimate agency that trains or represents children and make an appointment. Again, get references for anyone who will be working with your child. Teach your child that he may not respond to any casual contacts or "discovery" at the mall or other public place. Reputable agents don't approach children that way. Child predators do.

Perhaps the most frightening and insidious of the new ploys are contacts made by child predators through computer bulletin boards and "chat rooms." Bulletin board systems ("BBS") and chat rooms are operated by service providers such as America Online and Prodigy. A BBS is usually organized by topic or subject matter and can be accessed by subscribers to the service. Subscribers use their membership identification and log on to any BBS they select, where they can read messages left by other subscribers or type in their own messages. Chat rooms provide the same function except that typed messages are sent and received instantly, like an ongoing group conversation.

BBS and chat room services are an exciting and innovative way for people of all ages to "meet" on-line and share their interests and experiences. Most subscribers use made-up nicknames called "computer names" on the BBS and in chat rooms. Of course, there is no way of knowing with any certainty the true identity, age, sex, or other characteristics of anyone with whom you may be communicating through a BBS or chat room. And the anonymity and privacy afforded by these on-line encounters gives the sophisticated child predator a happy hunting ground for victims.

Any home computer with a modem and phone line and the appropriate software affords these molesters the opportunity to troll for child victims on-line. Many families now have computers with modems at home, and some children have their own computers in their bedrooms. Many school-age children know how to access bulletin boards and chat rooms on their computers. The clever predator knows and takes advantage of this. Once he establishes computer contact with a child on a BBS or in a chat room, he usually moves quickly toward his goal: arranging a real-life meeting with the child for sex.

Here's an example: Recently, a man using the computer name "Ken4Boys" used a computer chat room to establish contact with "a young boy" in another state. Ken started off easily, typing short messages to the boy inquiring about his interests and hobbies. But soon Ken turned to more personal topics: What do you look like? he typed to the boy. How big are you? Taking advantage of a child's natural curiosity about sex, Ken skillfully led the conversation into increasingly suggestive areas. Do you like massages? Full-body massages? Finally he offered to "do" the boy. On the computer or in person? the boy typed back. In person, Ken responded. He planned to visit the boy's hometown the following week, and he wanted to set up an in-person meeting. When the boy replied that he lived at home with his mother, Ken suggested, "Tell her you're going to the movies."

Ken arranged the meeting at a public park in the boy's hometown. How will I know you? the boy asked. Ken replied that he'd be wearing a baseball cap and sitting on a certain park bench. On the agreed day, Ken showed up wearing the baseball cap. He waited on the designated bench, anxiously looking around for his target. Finally Ken was met not by the compliant young boy he expected, but rather by a television news crew, which had staged the exposé. "Ken4Boys," it turned out, was a middle-aged man, a high-level executive with a publisher in another state. He was also a sophisticated, mobile sexual predator who had crossed the country hoping to entice a young boy into a sexual relationship. The episode was broadcast on television to educate parents about the dangers that can be lurking in computer BBS and chat rooms.

One law enforcement expert has commented that in most cases, like the "Ken4Boys" episode described above, the child who agrees to meet the molester in person has at least some idea of what the molester wants. But this doesn't mean that "it's the kid's fault" because he responded to the molester. As we know, children of all ages are curious about their bodies and about sex. This intensifies when the child matures and develops his own sex drive. The predator exploits this natural curiosity in attempting to entice the child into a situation that the child can't control. Children need to be educated about this potentially dangerous situation and taught how to avoid such entrapment. Nevertheless, as parents we need to remember: This is the predator's fault, not the child's; it is criminal; and it's extremely dangerous for the child.

Computer technology presents special opportunities to molesters, and special problems for parents. We want to encourage our children's exploration of this exciting and stimulating world, but we don't want them to be vulnerable to prowling predators. If your family has a computer for your child's use, experts recommend that you keep it in the family room or a place where all family members have access, especially when your child is elementary school age. Participate with your child in BBS and chat room conversations. If you aren't computer literate, let your child teach you the basics. You and your child should agree on which bulletin boards and chat rooms are okay for him to use. Stress that computer conversations are like a masquerade party. Your child doesn't really know whom he's talking to. He may think it's a child his own age, but it could be an adult pretending to be a child.

Rules for computer friendships should be established: Your child should not give his name, phone number, address, or personal information to anyone on the computer without your permission. And he should never, under any circumstances, agree to meet anyone in person without your consent. If any computer friend tries to violate these rules, or if any conversation makes your child uncomfortable (for example, someone wants to know what your child "looks like," or makes suggestive remarks), or if someone sends your child pornographic information or photos, he should terminate the contact immediately and notify you.

Teenagers may balk at having to share a computer in the family room. If they are permitted to keep a computer and modem in the privacy of their rooms, they must agree to abide by the rules described above. Almost every month, it seems, we see news accounts of sexual predators who try to set up meetings with children they've found on computer bulletin boards or chat rooms. Use these stories to remind your adolescent or teenager of the danger of agreeing to meet anyone that he knows only from computer contact. Once the child is alone with such a person, he is within that person's control—a very dangerous place for a child to be.

If the stranger molester has such an array of ploys for ensnaring children, what about the pal molester, whom the child and maybe even his parents already know and like? Clever pal molesters use a vast array of methods in their constant hunt for child victims. Experts say that these techniques can be devastating for their victims, but they are often very successful for the predators. According to detective Sergeant David Robshaw, Sexual Battery Squad of the Broward County (Florida) Sheriff's Office, "Child molesters tell me that the problem isn't *getting* child victims, it's *getting rid* of them when they mature out of the molester's preferred age range."

The pal molester is usually more socially adept, more subtle, more sophisticated, and every bit as dangerous as the stranger. This molester relies primarily on two carefully cultivated traits: his position of authority and access to children, and his own seductive skills.

The first step in this molester's plan is to secure regular access to a supply of potential victims: our children. Best of all is a position that provides not only access, but also authority and respectability in the child's world. Classic examples include the teacher, scout leader, coach, church youth group leader, music teacher, etc. Once the predator establishes his access and authority status, he immediately begins to exploit it.

A clever molester often starts with the child's parents. If he can deceive the parents into trusting him, they'll be more likely to permit or even encourage the child to spend time with him. The parents may invite the molester to the child's home, maybe even into the child's bedroom.

Exploiting his special status as teacher, coach, etc., the molester establishes a relationship with the parents that invites their trust and friendship. In so doing, he preys upon the parents' love for their child and their vulnerability to anyone who seems to share their affection for him. The molester shows interest in their child's progress, and he's willing to devote his own time and attention to "helping" their child. He recognizes how special the child is and offers suggestions and assistance for the parents, and perhaps special favors—extra tutoring or coaching, for example, free sports equipment or tickets to a special event. He's such a nice guy, they think. He really likes our child. But the molester has very specific goals: to lull the parents into a false sense of security, and to maintain close access to the potential victim.

The following example shows how powerful a weapon the parents' trust can be. A popular and charismatic man volunteered his time as youth leader for a Miami church. He was responsible, charming, and helpful to parents in the congregation, and everyone liked him. The outings and trips he arranged were well attended by youngsters in the church. But one young boy suddenly balked at attending a church-sponsored outing for kids, even though he previously had been fond of the youth leader. Over the child's objections, his annoyed father insisted that he take part in the event. After all, this was a church-sponsored trip with a "good Christian" who was devoted to youth ministry.

The boy reluctantly went on the trip. Soon afterward, the church youth leader was arrested and charged with molesting children—including the young boy—on that outing. The boy's resistance was his attempt to cope with his discomfort and instinctive recognition that something was "wrong" with the church youth leader. After this revelation, the boy's father was consumed with guilt and remorse. Yet parents will recognize that this clever molester had strong forces on his side. Clothed with the status of authority, respectability, and religious affiliation, he was able to gain the trust and support of the adults in the congregation; he exploited this to his advantage.

In another instance, the predator was a mental health professional who had targeted a young girl for seduction. How did he gain access to her? By hiring the child's mother as his secretary. The woman he hired, a struggling single mother, was grateful for the job. She had no idea of her boss's secret purpose. This clever predator— her boss—was always friendly and supportive. He began to feign romantic interest in the woman, and she was pleased. He was such a nice guy. Best of all, he seemed so fond of her daughter, so interested in the child's progress. The woman occasionally invited him to her home. Unknown to her, he exploited these opportunities to reconnoiter her home and, especially, her daughter's bedroom.

Once he had gained the woman's trust, he offered to keep an extra set of her house keys "in case of emergency." He used the keys one weekend when the woman and her child were out of town. Sneaking into their home like a burglar in the dead of night, he found his way to the child's bedroom and stole some of her underwear. Fortunately, this predator's plan was interrupted by law enforcement officials before he succeeded in molesting the child. But this well-educated professional man was willing to go to extraordinary lengths to achieve his goal.

Another example demonstrates the depths of a cynical molester's manipulation of trusting parents. In a well-publicized tragedy, a young boy went missing. The frantic parents recruited their friends and neighbors to help look for the child. Another "friend" offered to take care of the children of these volunteers while they searched for the missing boy. While the parents were gone, this man took advantage of his position of trust, and molested several of the children left in his care.

As discussed earlier, the pal molester is often very sophisticated at identifying and isolating a vulnerable child as a potential victim. Once he has chosen a target and, if possible, lulled the parents into a false sense of security, he begins his seduction of the child. This seduction mimics the seduction of an adult lover. He may start by giving special attention or privileges to the target child—a ride home after school, perhaps, or an invitation to his house for a get-together (with no other adults present). He concentrates on making the child feel important, special. He's never too busy to listen. He's always on the child's side, especially if there are tensions or problems between the child and his parents. Soon the child thinks of the molester as his special friend, his pal. He turns to the molester for emotional support, attention, and affection—exactly what the molester wants.

Sometimes a pal molester will manipulate one compliant child into unknowingly "recruiting" other victims for him. He may suggest that the child invite friends to a "party" at the molester's home, or on a trip or outing. Of course, the molester's purpose is to increase the number of victims he has access to. Sometimes child molesters "team up" with each other and share victims, as mentioned in the example of the Boy Scout leader earlier. Kenneth Lanning, supervisory special agent with the FBI, terms such arrangements "child sex rings." In this terminology, he includes day care center abuses and Satanic or religious cults that practice ritual child sexual abuse.

Once the pal molester begins to seduce his chosen victim, he works to overcome any inhibitions or reluctance about sexual activity that the child may have. Sometimes there is play—tickling, roughhousing—which provides the opportunity for "inadvertent" sexual touching. Or he may suggest activities like "playing doctor," swimming, or sports involving abbreviated clothing or changes of clothing. In one instance, "the nicest guy in the neighborhood" frequently offered to baby-sit young children in his home. Many busy parents accepted his "kind" offer. Once he was alone with the children, he encouraged them to take baths together and play in the nude. Meanwhile, he surreptitiously videotaped the children from hidden cameras that he controlled from a secret "command center" in his home.

The goal of such activities is to progress from nudity to fondling and sometimes full sexual contact. In this seduction process, the sophisticated molester will prey upon a child's natural curiosity about his own body and about sex. There may be erotic magazines or videotapes to desensitize the child. For example, an undercover federal agent recently seized an expertly made videotape knockoff of the *Flintstones* cartoon, in which the cartoon characters progressed from suggestive "play" to explicit sexual activity.

Child pornography is a favorite seduction tool for molesters. Experts say that 75 percent to 80 percent of the child pornography produced worldwide is consumed right here in the United States. Using photographs or videotapes of children engaged in sexual activity with adults or other children, the molester tells the child that this activity is okay, that "everyone does it," that it's fun, etc. He'll make sure that the sexual touching is pleasurable for the child—at least in the beginning. Does this feel good? he'll ask the child. Do you like this?

Sometimes the molester appeals to the child's desire to be more grown-up by saying, This is what adults do, and I'm treating you like an adult. Sometimes the pitch is a cynical appeal to the child's feelings for the molester. I've done so much for you, he tells the child. Won't you do this one little thing for me? Don't you want to please me? Don't you like me as much as I like you?

Once the molester has enticed the child into sexual contact, he often wants trophies, souvenirs, or photographs of the child in the act. He may take pictures or videotapes of the child naked or engaging in sexual contact with the molester or another child. These photographs are very valuable to the molester. As discussed earlier, he probably maintains an extensive collection of child pornography, which he uses to fantasize with and to trade with other molesters.

When he is actively engaged with a child victim, the molester also uses these photographs to further stimulate the child or to entice new victims. If a child becomes reluctant, he may use the pictures to blackmail the child into continuing the sexual activity or keeping the molester's "secret." Do you want me to show your parents these pictures? he asks the child. Do you want them to see you doing this? This can be a very effective coercive technique, especially if the child feels fearful or guilty about what's happened. Sometimes, when a child is reluctant to continue the abusive relationship, the molester may threaten him or a member of his family with physical harm or even death if he doesn't cooperate, or if he "tells."

The molester fears disclosure and prosecution, of course, but what he fears most is loss of access to child victims.

Many public schools, community agencies, and police departments now provide educational programs to teach children how to recognize and avoid child molesters and other dangers. Experts say these programs are helpful, especially if repeated frequently. Research demonstrates that these programs are most effective when parents participate and reinforce lessons at home with their children. Experts confirm that parents are the most important part of any prevention program.

Now that you recognize the child molester's methods, you can use the following suggestions to help protect your child.

1. Teach your child to ignore any adult's request for assistance unless the adult is a relative or a trusted adult. If your child feels threatened, he should run to a place of safety and call you.

2. Law enforcement specialists recommend that children should be taught not to go anywhere with a stranger, even if he threatens the child, or has a weapon, or tries to use force. When a child is physically threatened, the choices are all bad. But experts say the odds, such as they are, favor the child screaming, fighting, and running—anything but being abducted.

3. Don't put your child's name in a visible location on his clothes, toys, books, or backpack. When a stranger calls a child by name, the child may be caught off guard and more easily tricked into believing the stranger knows him or his parents.

4. Even when your child's name is not visible to a predator, your child might tell his name if asked by an adult. Tell your child not to give his name, your name, or your address or phone number to anyone without your permission.

5. Know what toys, books, sports equipment, and clothing your child owns, and keep track of legitimate gifts, borrowing from friends, etc.

6. If any adult offers you or your child "freebies"—free tickets, sports or electronic equipment, gifts, etc.—proceed with caution. Use your common sense and your knowledge of the adult and the circumstances to govern your judgment.

WHAT TO TELL YOUR CHILD AND HOW TO TELL HIM

Now we come to the crucial question: What should you tell your child about these dangers, and how?

Many parents, and even some educators, are reluctant to discuss these matters with children because they don't want to alarm them, or make them timid or fearful. We want childhood to be a time of innocence and freedom to explore. One mother remarked recently, "I know there's danger out there. But my four-year-old is such a friendly, trusting child, and I don't want to diminish that joy and innocence. I just don't want to upset her happy little world."

As a parent, of course you don't want to worry your child, but neither do you want him to be a naive target for predators. "Don't play the game of, We don't want to upset the children," says Don Ryce, father of Jimmy Ryce. "And don't say it can't happen here. That's just what the molester wants you to think."

So how can you protect your child without unduly frightening him? The subject of your child's safety is a serious one, but it doesn't have to be scary for him. You can teach your child all he needs to know to be safe and savvy without making him fearful of the world around him. The suggestions that follow will show you how to work with your child slowly and gently, over time, in an easy and appropriate way that takes advantage of natural learning opportunities. Most experts agree that a child's fears are likely to be diminished when parents discuss them and teach children some basic safety rules to follow. The goal is to protect your child by arming him with information and strategies to help keep him safe.

Of course, sound parenting skills are the foundation of any endeavor with your child. This means keeping the lines of communication open with your child, being involved in his interests and activities, knowing his friends and their parents, and keeping in touch with his teachers—in short, participating in your child's life in a meaningful way.

The first step in protecting your child is to be very clear about what it is that you want him to know. Specific suggestions about what to teach your child at different ages are set out below. Obviously, you will use different language and varying techniques with him as he grows. At each stage of childhood, there are certain developmental issues your child is dealing with. You must also keep these developmental issues in mind when you work with him.

When should you begin teaching your child about safety? The time is right now, whatever his age. Experts say that teaching your child to be safe is a continuous process, one that you'll be involved in as long as he's under your care. This process actually begins when our children are infants, when we try to keep them from harm by teaching them basic distinctions about what can hurt—what's hot, what's sharp, etc. So teaching your child to be savvy and aware of the dangers of molesters is an extension of the important work you've already begun.

Of course, different subjects and techniques are appropriate for your child at different ages, as described in the guidelines which follow. As you work through these guidelines, begin at the beginning, with the suggestions for the very youngest children, regardless of your own child's present age, and continue to the end. This will give you a comprehensive overview of the process of teaching your child to be safe. If you notice something that your child may have missed at an earlier age, you can make up for it now, using age-appropriate language and examples.

When should you talk to your child? First, take advantage of opportunities which occur naturally. For example, with a young child, bathing and dressing are opportunities to talk about our bodies and our right to privacy. If you observe a young child's discomfort with someone touching, kissing, or hugging him, it's a good time to discuss appropriate and inappropriate touching. For school-age children, the beginning of each school year is an occasion to establish safety rules for the coming year and review basic rules previously learned. When you are driving with your child, there's time to talk without the interruption of other activities. At home, a TV news story may provide an opportunity to discuss safety concerns. Watch for these natural opportunities and take advantage of them.

An especially important opportunity to talk to your child is in connection with a school-based child safety program. As mentioned earlier, these prevention programs are most effective when parents are involved. If your child's school has such a program, plan to participate as fully as possible. If not, consider working with your school board, PTA, or local police to establish one.

Sometimes you may need to set aside a special time to talk to your child. This doesn't have to take long, but you do need to get your child's attention for a few minutes without distractions. Most of the sample conversations included in this chapter are brief—three or four minutes at most. But each one is an example of how to address a safety topic in a forthright, nonthreatening manner. Before you have such a conversation with your child, plan what you want to say. Keep it simple, and keep it short.

Remember that developing and implementing a plan for child safety is an important part of your role as a parent, and it requires a continuing commitment of your time and effort. Once you have begun to teach your child the safety rules discussed here, together with appropriate prevention techniques and strategies to help keep him safe, you have a foundation upon which to build. But don't make the mistake of thinking that one conversation with your child, or one practice session, will take care of the situation. As your child matures, the safety issues will change, and your plan should be reevaluated frequently.

Once you've covered the basics, how often should you reinforce these lessons with your child? There is no set timetable, but we know that younger children need more frequent reminders. Again, use opportunities that occur naturally in your child's life—beginning each new school year, returning to school after vacations, beginning summer vacation, going to camp, etc. We know that children learn best through repetition and practice. Use these principles to your child's advantage.

What follows is a set of guidelines for parents to use. They are organized into two general categories: Basic Safety Rules for Children; and Key Concepts for Prevention. Basic Safety Rules are the "commonsense" instructions we give our children almost without thinking, such as, Don't go with anyone without a parent's permission. Key Concepts for Prevention address some specific strategies for protecting children from molesters. For example, we want to be sure our children know that they have a right to the privacy of their bodies, and that no one should violate this right. Again, you can teach these key concepts to your child without alarming or upsetting him.

To help parents in talking to children of different ages, the stages of childhood are arranged here in three basic groups: Preschool and Early Elementary School Age; Later Elementary School Age; and Adolescents and Teenagers. As part of the discussions of the first Safety Rule and the first Key Concept for Prevention, there are brief summaries of developmental considerations for each group, and then specific suggestions as to what to teach each age level. Some sample conversations with children of different ages are included, as well as some practice activities.

This is intended as a guide to help parents develop a plan for teaching what their child needs to know. It is expected that parents will modify these suggestions to fit their child's age, level of sophistication, and particular needs.

BASIC SAFETY RULES FOR CHILDREN

- Don't talk to strangers. "Stranger" means anyone you don't know.
- Don't go with anyone without a parent's permission.
- If someone approaches you, say no, then go.
- In case of emergency, go only with a trusted adult.
- Let your parents know where you are at all times.
- Don't go out alone. Use the buddy system.
- Follow danger instincts.
- Secrets can be dangerous. Don't keep secrets from your parents.

Remember that even very young children know that we want them to obey certain safety rules: Only food goes in your mouth—not toys, dirt, etc. Hold a parent's hand when out in public. Don't cross the street without a parent. Don't approach a strange animal. You have probably told your child such rules many times, and maybe you've given specific reasons for them. "Don't touch that because it's hot. It might burn you. It would hurt."

In our rush to protect our children, however, we sometimes forget to remind them of the reason for *all* the rules: We want them to be safe because we love them very much. Experts say that children of all ages need to be reminded of our love and affection for them, and our acceptance of them just the way they are.

The safety rules which follow are arranged in sequence to help parents decide which concepts to introduce to their child at different ages. The goal is to establish a foundation of basic safety rules at the youngest ages, with reinforcement and age-appropriate modifications as your child grows. Remember that all the basic safety rules really apply to children of all ages. Teaching your child to be safe is a continuous, dynamic process which evolves over time. What follows is not a rigid time-line approach, but rather a sequence through which you and your child will move at your own pace.

DON'T TALK TO STRANGERS. "STRANGER" MEANS ANYONE YOU DON'T KNOW.

Whatever your child's age, this is the place to start. We've all told our children, "Don't talk to strangers." But as we've seen, this advice doesn't help when the child is approached by the friendly man in the park looking for his puppy, or the "officer" who wants to "help" the child, or even the handsome, charming young man with the cast on his arm. To a child, "a stranger" in this context is someone with horns, a monster, a bogey man, not the friendly, nice-looking man playing video games next to him at the mall. But it is this very dichotomy that child molesters exploit in order to deceive their victims.

What should a parent do? Begin now by telling your child that "a stranger" is not necessarily someone who looks or acts scary. Rather, a stranger is anyone who is not a *known adult*—a relative, friend, teacher, etc., who is a *regular* part of the child's life. Stress that your child should not talk to *anyone* he doesn't know who approaches him, no matter how attractive, pleasant, and friendly that person may seem. As an analogy, you could remind your child that most dogs are friendly to children, but some are not. Sometimes we can't tell by looking at a strange dog whether it might bite a child. That's why we follow a safety rule: Stay away from strange animals.

Teach your child that adults are not supposed to ask children for help with their problems. Adults should only ask other adults to assist them. This means that if an adult approaches your child and asks for any kind of help—looking for a lost puppy, choosing a toy or pet, asking for directions, carrying packages, whatever—your child should immediately be alert to a situation in which a seemingly "nice" adult could be dangerous. This is especially true if the adult wants your child to go somewhere with him. Your child should ignore any adult's request for assistance and simply go on about his business. If the child feels threatened, he should yell, "Keep away from me!" and then run to a place of safety.

If your child follows this rule, might he seem rude to an adult? Perhaps, in some circumstances, this behavior could appear rude. But so what? Your child's safety is more important than any adult's opinion of his manners. And we adults have to accept that the rules are different now from when we were growing up. These days, it's simply too dangerous to expect a child to differentiate between "good" adults and clever child predators when strangers ask for a child's help.

Preschool and Early Elementary School Age Children:

An important developmental task at this age is learning physical independence, beginning with self-care skills such as dressing, feeding, and grooming. Children need structured situations and limitations, but also some freedom to explore under the supervision of adult caretakers. Children interact mostly with family, caretakers chosen by a parent, and peers and teachers at school. It's up to parents to be sure the adults they choose to spend time with their children are safe.

What to Teach:

Generally, your child should know his full name, address, and phone number. He should know how to call 911 in a home emergency and be able to give appropriate, accurate information. If you have speed-dial, show your child how to use it. If not, have the child practice calling 911 and giving necessary information.

Children should not be alone in public at this age. A parent or trusted adult should accompany the child to a public restroom. If your child becomes separated from you or lost in a shopping mall or store, he should go to the nearest sales counter, get an employee's attention, and report the necessary information. This needs to be practiced until it's automatic. When children and even adults are upset and under stress, they're likely to forget things.

Here's a sample conversation with a preschool girl:

Parent: I want to talk to you about some safety rules. Do you know what rules are?

Child: I don't know.

Parent: Rules tell us what we should do. Do you remember when I was making cookies and you wanted to take one off the cookie sheet?

Child: You told me not to touch it.

Parent: That's right. I told you not to touch the cookie. Do you know why I said that?

Child: Because it was hot. I could get burned.

Parent: That's right. That's a safety rule. Don't touch anything hot because you might get burned. Can you tell me another rule that you know?

Child: Hold your hand when we cross the street.

Parent: Very good. That's right. That's another safety rule. Now, do you know why we have these rules?

Child: So I won't get hurt.

Parent: Right. So you won't get hurt. I want you to be safe and happy. Do you know why?

Child: Because you love me.

Parent: That's right! Because I love you more than anything. I want you always to be safe and happy. Now I want to tell you about another other safety rule. It's an easy one: Don't talk to strangers.

Child: O.K.

Parent: Do you know what a stranger is?

Child: Somebody I don't know.

Parent: That's right. What does a stranger look like?

Child: A mean, scary person. A bad man.

Parent: Could a stranger look like a nice person?

Child: A nice person isn't really a stranger.

Parent: No, that's not right. A stranger could look nice. He could act nice, too, but he's still a stranger. Remember what a stranger is?

Child: Oh, yeah. A stranger is somebody I don't know.

Parent: So if somebody comes up to you and you don't know him, is he a stranger?

Child: Yes, he's a stranger.

Parent: Even if he's smiling and he looks nice?

Child: He's still a stranger.

Parent: What if he tells you his name? Is he still a stranger?

Child: I don't know.

Parent: I'll tell you. He's still a stranger even if he tells you his name. Maybe you know his name, but you don't know *him*. And I don't know him, either. So if he tries to talk to you, what should you do?

Child: I don't talk to him. I don't talk to strangers.

Parent: Very good! That's the rule. You don't talk to strangers, no matter how nice they seem. Now let me ask you a question. What if the stranger came up to you in the park and asked you to help him look for his puppy? What should you do?

Child: I don't talk to him because he's a stranger.

Parent: What if he tells you his name and he seems nice? What if he has a picture of his cute little puppy and he says, please help me find my lost puppy?

Child: I don't talk to him.

Parent: What if he asks you to look around the park with him?

Child: I don't talk to him. And I don't go with him, because he's a stranger.

Parent: Good for you!

This format can be varied to suit your child's age and level of knowledge. Use this example to structure your conversations with your child about the basic safety rules.

Later Elementary School Age Children:

Children continue to be concerned about developing independence. They need less structure now and can solve simple social problems, often using trial-and-error techniques. Children understand simple explanations and can identify the viewpoints of others. They are concerned with the present more than the past and have difficulty projecting into the future. Children depend upon the family for socialization, but now they have more peer relationships in school and outside activities. Parents still must make sure the adults their children spend time with are safe.

What To Teach:

Children of this age can accompany parents or relatives or trusted adults to shopping malls, amusement parks, or video arcades without constant supervision. The adult in charge should always set a meeting place and time in case the child becomes lost or separated from the group.

Sometimes a child may be home alone for a short time. He should be taught not to let anyone know his parents aren't there. He should not answer the door when he's alone, except for a relative or trusted adult.

Here's a sample conversation with a fifth-grade boy:

Parent: There's a safety rule I want to talk to you about. But first, I have a question for you. Has an adult ever asked you to help him do something?

Child: My teacher asked me to help clean the chalkboard.

Parent: What did you do?

Child: I helped him.

Parent: That's fine, because that's your teacher. Has an adult that you don't know—a stranger—ever asked you to help him?

Child: I don't know. Like what?

Parent: Like a man who stops his car beside the sidewalk and asks you for directions. A man you don't know. Has that ever happened to you?

Child: No.

Parent: What would you do if that happened?

Child: Well, I guess if I knew the place, I'd give him the directions.

Parent: I don't want you to do that. There's something I think would be safer for you to do. If you don't know him, just ignore him and go on your way. Stay away from the car.

Child: Why?

Parent: Because sometimes strangers pretend to be lost and ask kids for directions. Then if the kid comes close to the car, the stranger might grab him and pull him inside.

Child: That would never happen to me.

Parent: Why not?

Child: Because I'm pretty strong. I wouldn't let anybody pull me inside a car.

Parent: I'm glad you wouldn't let anybody do that. But it could happen so fast that you didn't have time to resist. Some time maybe you and I can test this with my car, okay?

Child: Whatever.

Parent: Anyway, I want to talk to you about a safety rule. If a stranger asks you for any kind of help, just ignore him and go on your way. Stay away from him. If you feel threatened, run to a safe place and call me or Dad. O.K.?

Child: I thought I was supposed to be helpful to adults.

Parent: I like it when you are helpful to adults that we know and trust. I don't want you to try to be helpful to other adults. It's not safe. Adults shouldn't be asking kids for help anyway. Adults should ask for help from other adults, not kids.

Child: All right.

Parent: What if you were at the mall and a man asked you for help? Suppose he asked you to come to his car and look at a video game he bought for his son? What should you do?

Child: Would he give me a game, too?

Parent: What??!!

Child: Just kidding. I would ignore him. If he kept on bothering me, I'd go find a phone and call you. O.K.?

Parent: O.K.!

Adolescents and Teenagers:
Children of this age are striving for independence from their parents. They frequently test limits and are often in conflict with parents over rules they consider too strict. They are very concerned with their appearance, and they respond much more to peer influence than to parental control. This makes them especially vulnerable to manipulations like the "I'm going to make you a star" routine, which was discussed previously. Adolescents and teenagers understand cause and effect, and they want to exercise their own judgment. But they often take irresponsible risks out of a desire to belong to the group, or a misguided sense of their own invincibility. They have difficulty imagining that anything bad could really happen to them.

What to Teach:
Remember that all the basic safety rules described here apply even to adolescents and teenagers, modified appropriately to suit the child's age, experience, and growing independence. Older children may begin to balk at these restrictions, but parents should remain firm. There will probably be many areas of disagreement between you and your child as he moves into adolescence, when children are especially resentful of what they consider to be authoritarian pronouncements and strict rules. You can compromise with your child on other issues—curfew, clothes, grooming, hair, etc.—but insist on compliance with safety rules. Secretly, your child may even like this. It sets clear limits and lets him know how much his parents care about him. It's also a convenient, face-saving way for a child to get out of a difficult situation. Your child can always say, "My parents won't let me. They're so mean!" Let him blame it on you. It's your job to be cautious where his safety and welfare are concerned.

Here's a sample conversation with a teenage girl:

Parent: Where are you going?
Child: I'm going to the mall with my friends.
Parent: Who?

Child: Tiffany, Lisa, and Amber.

Parent: Who's driving?

Child: I am. I mean, may I?

Parent: Yes, you may. Which mall are you going to?

Child: Crosstown.

Parent: That reminds me. Did you see that news story on TV yesterday? About something that happened at the Crosstown Mall?

Child: No. I have to go now. My friends are waiting for me.

Parent: I want to talk to you about this. It will only take a minute, and then you can go.

Child: O.K.

Parent: Some teenage girls were at the mall and a man came up to them. Someone they didn't know. He said he was a talent scout and he asked them if they'd like to be on MTV.

Child: Cool!

Parent: Not cool. He wasn't really a talent scout and he had nothing to do with MTV. But he flattered the girls and asked them to come with him to an audition at a studio. He said he would drive them there.

Child: Uh-oh. What happened?

Parent: The girls all agreed to go with him. Fortunately, it turned out that he was a TV reporter and they were taping this for a show to warn people about child molesters. But if he had really been a molester, those girls would have been in danger.

Child: But nothing happened. Can I go now?

Parent: In a minute. The point is, even though these girls are teenagers, they could still be tricked by a clever stranger. You know—

Child: I know. Don't talk to strangers. I remember.

Parent: I don't think something like this would happen to you and your friends, but I want to be sure you know what to do.

Child: I know what to do.

Parent: Good. Just remember that people aren't always who

they seem to be. Even someone who seems friendly and charming could be dangerous. The safest thing to do is—

Child: Don't talk to strangers. I know, Mom. Bye.

DON'T GO WITH ANYONE WITHOUT A PARENT'S PERMISSION.

Your child should be taught not to go with *anyone* without your permission. Even though your child has learned the fundamental safety rule about not talking to strangers, he could be approached by someone who is not, strictly speaking, a stranger, but who could be dangerous. There may be many adults in your child's life that he knows by name or sight, but who are not well-known to you. Don't leave your child in the position of having to decide whether to trust such an adult who asks him to go somewhere. This leaves him vulnerable to a clever predator who uses a ruse such as pretending to have your permission to pick him up from school.

Establish a safety rule and make it explicit: Your child is not to go with *anyone* unless you tell him he can.

Here's a sample conversation with a preschool boy:

Parent: I want to talk to you about a safety rule. Do you remember when we talked about rules before?

Child: I'm not supposed to talk to strangers. A stranger is anyone I don't know.

Parent: That's right. I'm glad you remember that rule. Now I want to tell you another safety rule.

Child: O.K.

Parent: Here's the rule: Never go with anyone but Daddy [or Grandma, etc.] or me, unless I say you can. That's a rule. O.K.?

Child: What about my teacher?

Parent: Right. I say that you can go with your teacher. So going with your teacher is following the rule. O.K.?

Child: O.K.

Parent: Let's practice following the safety rule. What if a man comes to your school and asks you to go with him?

Child: I don't go.

Parent: That's right. That's following the rule. You don't go with him, no matter who he is. Now, what if a woman comes to your school and says I told her to pick you up? What should you do?

Child: If you said I could, I would go with her.

Parent: But did *I* tell *you* to go with her?

Child: No.

Parent: No. *I* didn't tell *you* to go with her. So what should you do?

Child: I don't go.

Parent: That's right. You don't go with her. That's following the rule. What if you know her? What should you do?

Child: I don't go because you didn't tell me to.

Parent: Very good! What if she knows your name?

Child: I don't go with her.

Parent: That's right. That's following the rule. I think you really know this rule.

IF SOMEONE APPROACHES YOU, SAY NO, THEN GO.

Your child should be taught what he should do if he is approached by an unauthorized person: Say no, then go, and find a parent or trusted adult and tell what happened.

Young children may not understand that they have the right to say no to an adult who asks them to do something. Give your child permission and explicit instructions about when and how to say no to an adult who wants to take him somewhere. With young children, it may be helpful to rehearse and practice this rule.

Even older children, adolescents, and teenagers should be

reminded that if they ever feel threatened by someone, they should make a commotion, attract public attention, and then get away quickly.

Sample conversation with a preschool boy:

Parent: Remember when we talked about how you don't go with anyone unless I say you can?

Child: Yes. That's a safety rule.

Parent: Good for you. I'm glad you remember that rule. Now I'll tell you another safety rule. There's something you should do if someone tries to get you to go with him, and I didn't say you could. Here's what I want you to do. Say no, then go. Can you say that?

Child: Say no, then go.

Parent: Right. Say no, then go. Here is what that means. First, you should tell the person no. Say it in a loud voice so I can hear you.

Child: No!

Parent: That's good and loud. Then you *go*. That means you go find your teacher or me or Daddy and tell us what happened. O.K.? That's a rule. Say no, then go. Tell me the rule.

Child: Say no, then go.

Parent: Right. Now, let me see you practice following that rule. Pretend that a man comes to our door right now and asks you to go with him. Show me how you follow the rule.

IN CASE OF EMERGENCY, GO ONLY WITH A TRUSTED ADULT.

Establish a family plan for emergencies. Your child is already familiar with school emergency plans such as fire drills. Build upon this knowledge.

A parent might say something like this: "It's important to plan what we should do in case of emergency. There are different kinds of emergencies everyone should be prepared for. We're going to plan what we should do in emergencies and then we're going to practice, just as you practice fire drills at school." Next, review what your child should do in case of a medical emergency at home. If something happens to an adult home alone with a child, the child should know how to call for help.

What if you have an automobile accident or other emergency while your child is at school? Tell your child *exactly* what would happen. Name a trusted adult—Aunt Sue or Grandma or Mrs. Smith, the next-door neighbor—who would call your child's teacher or go pick him up. Identify a list of trusted adults *by name.* Be sure you have some backups ready in case your first choice isn't available. Your child should *not* rely on his own judgment as to whether to trust an adult, even an adult he thinks he knows. Only *you* can tell him which adults to trust when you're not there. Be sure he knows the names of trusted adults and review the list with him frequently. He should know the phone number of at least one trusted adult.

Since the "emergency" ruse is fairly common with child predators, discuss this situation specifically. A stranger might approach your child and say, "Your mother's been hurt in an accident! She sent me to take you to the hospital. Come with me!" The stranger might even know the child's name. The child, confused and worried, might accompany the adult unless he has been trained in exactly what to do. Stress that your child should not leave school or get in a car with anyone else without your permission, no matter what. If the child is approached by someone else—even someone wearing a badge or uniform—the child should refuse to go. Then he should go to a trusted adult or call home for assistance.

Your family plan for emergencies should *not* include a "code word" to designate a genuine emergency. Although this practice has sometimes been advised in the past, experts now say that using a code word can be dangerous since it's relatively easy to manipulate children into divulging the word.

Sample conversation with a fourth-grade girl:

Parent: I want to talk to you about what to do if I had an emergency while you were at school. Have you ever wondered about that?

Child: Not really. I guess someone would come to pick me up.

Parent: That's right, someone would. I want you to know exactly what would happen, and what you should do if I had any kind of emergency while you were at school. Think of this as a kind of fire drill. You have fire drills at school, right?

Child: Yes, we do.

Parent: How often do you have fire drills?

Child: Once a month. But we've never had a real fire.

Parent: But you still have fire drills, right? Why?

Child: So we can practice what to do in case there ever was a real fire.

Parent: What are you supposed to do?

Child: Line up at the door and follow the teacher outside.

Parent: Good. Now let's talk about what you should do if I'm in an accident or something while you're at school. I would have Grandma [or Aunt Sue or whoever] call the school. Then Grandma would come to pick you up.

Child: What if Grandma couldn't come?

Parent: If Grandma couldn't come, Aunt Sue would be there. There are only certain adults that I trust to take care of you if I can't be there. They are [list the trusted adults by name].

Child: O.K.

Parent: Let's write this out together. I'll make a list and then you copy it.

Child: O.K.

Parent: I'm going to give this list of trusted adults to your teacher so she'll know who is allowed to pick you up if I'm not there. And I'll remind you once in a while about the list, O.K.?

Child: O.K.

Parent: What if someone else comes to your school and says that your mom's been in an accident and wants you to go with him? What should you do?

Child: Say no, then go tell the teacher.

Parent: Good. Now, what if a man wearing a uniform or a badge asks you to come with him?

Child: Go talk to my teacher.

Parent: Right. What if he knows your name?

Child: Same thing. Go tell the teacher. Then call home.

Parent: What if I'm not home?

Child: Call Grandma [or whoever].

Parent: Good for you!

LET YOUR PARENTS KNOW WHERE YOU ARE AT ALL TIMES.

As our children grow up, we allow them to venture outside the home more with friends and family members. Gradually we permit them to arrange some of their own activities and make their own plans. But even with older children, parents need to know where their child is at all times. And he may only go where a parent gives him permission to go, no matter how old he is.

Teach your child that it is his responsibility to comply with this rule and keep you informed of his whereabouts. If the child's plans change, he should always come home or call parents *first* for permission. Be sure your child knows how to use a pay phone to call home. This is a good time to reinforce previously taught rules, especially not going with someone without parental permission.

DON'T GO OUT ALONE. USE THE BUDDY SYSTEM.

Preschool and early elementary school age children should not be alone in public. Experts say that young children should be accompanied by a parent or trusted adult when they go outside the home. Older children, adolescents, and teenagers should not be alone in public more than absolutely necessary. Obviously, older children don't have to be supervised by an adult every minute, but they should practice the buddy system in public.

Law enforcement experts remind us that predators look for the most physically vulnerable child—the child alone at the playground, the child walking alone, or riding his bike alone. Make sure your child doesn't fall into this vulnerable category.

FOLLOW DANGER INSTINCTS.

Teach your child to trust his own instinctive warnings of danger. We've all had the experience of feeling suddenly uncomfortable around someone, or taking an instant, inexplicable dislike to someone. Ask your child if he's ever had that experience. Did someone make him feel uncomfortable or "creepy"? Maybe an adult was standing too close to the child, invading his private space. Or maybe it was just a sense of something wrong with the person.

When this happens, your child should pay attention to his feelings and get away as quickly as possible. He should *not* argue with himself about it, make excuses for the person, or let anyone change his mind. He shouldn't wait until the person "does something." He doesn't have to say anything to anyone. He just has to leave.

We know that these instincts are very powerful and deeply ingrained in us. Several young women who were approached by Ted Bundy later reported that they felt these instinctive warnings about him. Those who heeded their feelings are still alive today. These danger instincts are literally lifesaving. Teach your child to recognize and respect his own instinctive warnings about people and situations.

Sample conversation with an eighth-grade girl:

Parent: There's something I want to talk to you about.

Child: Not again!

Parent: This is something I've been thinking about and I want to be sure you know it. Do you know what instincts are?

Child: Like birds migrating south in the winter?

Parent: That's not exactly what I meant. Have you ever felt creepy around someone even though you didn't know exactly why? Or have you ever felt the hair stand up on the back of your neck when you were frightened?

Child: Yeah, I guess so.

Parent: That's the kind of instinct I'm talking about. The kind that warns you about danger, even if you don't understand what the danger is.

Child: O.K., I get it.

Parent: Have you ever felt that way about a person?

Child: Yeah, I have. There's this guy at school who gives me the creeps.

Parent: How does he make you feel?

Child: Icky, and sort of self-conscious. I'm kind of scared of him. I don't like to be around him.

Parent: That's exactly what I mean. Does he do something that makes you feel this way?

Child: Not really. He's just creepy. Well, I don't like the way he looks at me. He sort of stares at me.

Parent: What do you do when you feel this way?

Child: I stay away from him. I find my friends and we go off together.

Parent: Good for you. That's just what I want you to do. Listen to your own warnings about people. Your instincts. Then stay away from anyone who gives you that creepy feeling. You don't have to wait until someone does something wrong. As soon as you get that feeling, that's a warning. Get away from that person.

SECRETS CAN BE DANGEROUS. DON'T KEEP SECRETS FROM YOUR PARENTS.

Of course, we all keep secrets such as a special gift or surprise for a family member or friend. These are happy secrets that we eventually get to tell. And close friends may share confidences that aren't told to anyone else.

But some secrets are dangerous. A dangerous secret makes the child worried or unhappy. A dangerous secret is one that an adult asks a child to keep from his parents. This ploy is often used by child molesters to conceal the molestation and isolate the child victim from the protection of his parents and caring adults. Teach your child that whenever anyone (other than a parent or trusted adult) asks him to keep a secret from you, he should refuse and tell you immediately.

The Basic Safety Rules for Children which you have just read are general, "commonsense" rules for child safety. In addition to these basic safety rules, parents need to understand some Key Concepts for Prevention described below. The goal is to instill in your child certain concepts about himself, his body, and his rights which will help protect and preserve his physical and emotional well-being.

KEY CONCEPTS FOR PREVENTION

- Your child has a right to the privacy of his body.
- If someone tries to violate this right, he should yell and tell.
- If someone violates this right, it's not the child's fault.
- People who seem good can sometimes do bad things.

Many parents are uncomfortable with the idea of sex education for their children. They worry that warning their children about the dangers of molesters requires delving into explicit details about sex, perversions, etc., which they feel are inappropriate for discussion with their children. But it doesn't have to be that way. You can teach your child what he needs to know to protect himself from molesters without going into all this information. What you really need to teach your child is summarized in the Key Concepts for Prevention. As you will see, these concepts can be taught to your child in a non-threatening way that doesn't interfere with parents' concerns and beliefs.

YOUR CHILD HAS A RIGHT TO THE PRIVACY OF HIS BODY. IF SOMEONE TRIES TO VIOLATE THIS RIGHT, HE SHOULD YELL AND TELL.

It's a fact that people are sexual beings from birth to death. We know that children have a natural curiosity about their bodies and sex, a curiosity that increases in adolescence and the teenage years. As a parent, your goal is to establish yourself as someone with whom your child can discuss these things. This makes him less vulnerable to the advances of a molester, more able to stand up for his rights, and more likely to tell you if someone approaches him or actually molests him.

Preschool and Early Elementary School Age Children:
Very young children are naturally curious about bodies—their own, their siblings', their parents'. For them, this subject is exciting and important. They are proud of their bodies and interested in their individual differences, including gender differences. They may like having attention paid to their bodies and showing off, maybe even their private parts. They find a parent's touch pleasurable. Experts say this is natural and normal for very young children.

Parents usually teach their children to be modest about their bodies, especially their private parts. This training should begin early, in a casual and natural manner, with recognizing and discussing the child's body parts and the physical differences between the sexes. Just as we teach children the names for their facial features and other body parts, we give names to the sex organs.

Experts recommend that parents teach their children the proper names for sex organs—penis, vagina, breasts—rather than using euphemisms. Many parents are not comfortable doing this. They prefer to call the sex organs "your private parts" or some other name. Use whatever terms you are comfortable with. Remember that you want to teach concepts in a relaxed, nonthreatening way. You don't want to make your child fearful or uncomfortable about his body, or his own exploration of it. We know this is a natural and normal part of childhood, as is a certain amount of "playing doctor" with young age-mates.

What to Teach:
Remember that even at these young ages, you want to begin teaching your child the concepts listed on the previous page. First, your child has a right to the privacy of his body, especially his sex organs. He alone should decide when and with whom he shares his body. This includes physical expressions of affection such as hugging and kissing, and touching in general. Show your child that you respect his right to the privacy of his body, and that you insist that others respect his right, too.

Second, no one should violate the child's right to bodily privacy. This means that no one may look at or touch the child's private parts without his permission. Children must be taught explicitly that they may—and should—refuse anyone's request to do this. They should also refuse to look at or touch the sex organs of another person. With young children, some experts advise teaching the child to "yell and tell" if someone asks him to do this. This means that if any adult tries to look at or touch the child's private parts, or asks the child to look at or touch the adult's, the child should refuse loudly and then tell his parents immediately.

Of course, there are commonsense exceptions to this rule. In cleaning or bathing a young child, a parent may touch his sex organs. A doctor or nurse also may do so for medical reasons. What should be stressed is that *no other person* should do this.

In talking with your child about this in a natural, nonthreatening way, you are letting him know that this is a subject that he can talk to you about. You are the first person he should turn to.

Sample conversation with a preschool girl:

Parent: When you were a baby, I fed you and dressed you and changed your diapers. But you're a big girl now. You don't need to have me do those things for you.

Child: Sometimes I need help with my buttons.

Parent: That's right. And you can tell me, "I need help with my buttons." But when you can do it yourself, you can tell me, "Thank you, but I can do it myself."

Child: I can go to the bathroom by myself, too.

Parent: If you don't need any help in the bathroom, you can tell me. It's O.K. if you want some privacy. Your body is your own and *you* can say who touches it.

Child: I like you to touch me when you hug me and kiss me.

Parent: I like it, too. But if someone tries to hug you or kiss you or touch you and you don't like it, you should say, "Don't do that." O.K.?

Child: O.K. I don't like to kiss Uncle Paul when he comes over.

Parent: I didn't know that. I'm glad you told me. You don't have to kiss Uncle Paul if you don't want to. Do you feel like shaking hands with him instead?

Child: Yes, that would be O.K.

Parent: I'll tell Uncle Paul, O.K.?

Child: O.K.

Parent: Some parts of your body are very private. Do you know which parts they are?

Child: My vagina and my breasts.

Parent: That's right. Your vagina and your breasts. Those are the parts that we keep covered in public. If someone tries to look at or touch those parts, you should say, "Leave me alone!" Then you should tell me right away.

Child: All right.

Parent: That is a rule. Remember when we talked about rules before?

Child: Yes, I remember. I don't go with anyone unless you tell me I can.

Parent: Good for you. That's right. Now you have another rule to remember. If someone tries to look at or touch your private parts, you should say, "Leave me alone!" Then you should tell me right away.

Child: O.K.

Parent: Here's a saying to help you remember the rule. "Yell and tell." Can you say that?

Child: Yell and tell.

Parent: "Yell and tell" means you yell, "Leave me alone!" and then you tell me right away. Let me hear you yell, "Leave me alone!"

Child: Leave me alone!

Parent: Good for you. What do you do next?

Child: Tell you right away.

Parent: That's right. Yell and tell. It's a good rule.

Later Elementary School Age Children:

Now it's time to be more explicit about child molesters. Building upon the foundation above, expand your discussion to include that "someone" who might want to look at or touch your child's private parts, or ask your child to look at his. Remember that you don't want to alarm your child or make him fearful or uncomfortable. It's important to remind him how much you love him and want him to be safe. Stress that we have safety rules for many situations, and now you want to discuss a particular situation. Maintain your matter-of-fact approach and reinforce the idea that your child can talk to you about these things. It might be a little embarrassing or uncomfortable for both of you, but that's O.K. This is important work.

What to Teach:

At this point, your child should know that it's wrong for an adult to look at or touch a child's sex organs, or to ask the child to look at or touch his. Now it's time to stress that this is not only wrong, it's against the law. An adult who looks at or touches a child's sex organs, or tries to get a child to look at or touch his sex organs, is called "a molester."

Your child may ask why an adult would do this. You could say something like this: "We don't really know why some adults want to do this, but it's wrong and they know it's wrong. They have a problem. It's their problem, not yours. They should get help, but they shouldn't involve you in their problem."

Remind your child that no adult should ask him to take his clothes off or take pictures of him without clothes. If someone tries to do any of these things, your child should follow the same rule he learned earlier: He should refuse to go with the person, then go to a safe place and report the incident to you or another trusted adult.

Sample conversation with a fourth-grade boy:

Parent: Remember the safety rules we've talked about?

Child: Yes. I have to let you know where I am all the time. I'm not supposed to go with any adult unless you say I can.

Parent: Right. We also talked about what would happen if I'm in an accident or something while you're at school.

Child: We made up a list of adults that you trust to take care of me. I'm not supposed to go with anyone else.

Parent: Good. You know we have these rules because I love you very much and I want you to be safe.

Child: Yeah, I know.

Parent: Now I want to talk to you about another situation that we have rules about. Remember when we talked about the private area of your body?

Child: Yes.

Parent: I told you that no adult should look at or touch your penis, or ask you to look at or touch his penis. Remember?

Child: I remember.

Parent: You know that if someone does that, it's wrong. Now I want to give you some more information about that. It's not just wrong for someone to do that, it's against the law. A person who does that is called a "molester." Have you ever heard that word?

Child: I think so. Is that a child molester?

Parent: Yes.

Child: I've heard that word but I didn't really know what it meant.

Parent: Now you know what a child molester is. It's someone who looks at or touches a child's sex organs, or asks the child to look at or touch his sex organs. A child molester is committing a crime when he does this, and he knows it. All adults know that this is against the law.

Child: Why would someone want to do that?

Parent: Even doctors and psychologists don't really know why some people do this. But it's wrong, and the molester knows that it's wrong. The molester has a problem, but it's *his* problem. It's not *your* problem. There's only one thing you have to do.

Child: I know. Say no, then tell you. That's two things.

Parent: You're so smart!

Adolescents and Teenagers:

At this age, your child is undergoing enormous physical and emotional changes, which can be unsettling for the entire family. Remember that your guidance is even more important now. Let your child know that you're available to talk to him about anything. Keep the lines of communication open, even if this requires extra effort and patience on your part.

What to Teach:

By now, your child should know and understand the basics about child molesters. You need to remind him that adolescents and teenagers are just as likely to be approached by molesters as younger children are. Just because he's older now, and striving for independence, doesn't mean that this can't happen to him.

You may have to plan how to approach your child about this subject. Children at this age are especially sensitive to anything they interpret as a lecture from parents. It may be helpful to use a news story about molestation to broach the subject. Remind your child that he should say no to anyone who wants to involve him in this conduct, even if it's someone he knows and likes. Your child may be concerned about "telling on" someone he likes, or "getting them in trouble." You should stress that if that person gets in trouble, it's not the child's fault. That person is a molester, and the molester knows what he's doing is wrong. The molester should get treatment for his problem so that he won't continue to victimize others.

Again, you don't want to alarm your child or imply that all sexual contact is wrong. You are teaching your child about the dangers of a specific situation, the child molester. He's not too old to need reminding.

Sample conversation with an eighth-grade boy:

Parent: Did you see this story in the paper? It's about a junior high band teacher who was molesting girls in the band.

Child: Yeah, I saw it.

Parent: It's frightening to me to know that someone like that is teaching in our schools. I worry that you might come into contact with someone like that.

Child: Don't worry about it.

Parent: But I do worry about it. I'm entitled to. I'm your mother and I love you. I want you to be safe, and it's my job to be concerned about these things.

Child: That isn't going to happen to me.

Parent: Why do you say that?

Child: Because I'm a boy.

Parent: Maybe you didn't know that boys are often the target of child molesters. In fact, experts say that many boys are molested.

Child: I know how to take care of myself.

Parent: I'm glad that you do. But molestation isn't something that just happens to little kids. Someone could try to molest you or one of your friends. These girls in the band were about your age. I'll bet they didn't think anything like this could happen to them, either.

Child: O.K., O.K.

Parent: Anybody could be a molester. A stranger, or even someone you know, like a teacher or coach. I don't think this will happen to you, but I want you to know what to do just in case.

Child: Please stop. I know what to do.

Parent: Good. Then just tell me so I'll know that you know.

Child: O.K. First, I tell them I don't want to do that. I don't let anybody manipulate me or con me into doing something I don't want to do, no matter who it is. I won't do anything that makes me feel creepy. Then I get away from them.

Parent: Then?

Child: Then I tell someone.

Parent: Who?

Child: You.

Parent: Right. If you can't tell me for some reason, tell your dad or some other adult that you trust. Right?

Child: O.K.

IF SOMEONE VIOLATES THIS RIGHT, IT'S NOT THE CHILD'S FAULT.

You want your child to tell you immediately if someone makes an attempt to molest him, or actually does molest him. It's essential that your child understand that if molestation does happen, it's not his fault, no matter what. You will always love him, and you'll always take his side. Molestation is always the fault of the molester. There are no exceptions.

As we know, experts say that many—perhaps even the majority—of child molestations go unreported. This is very unfortunate because keeping molestation a secret creates big problems for a child. First, the child is deprived of the love and emotional support that his parents or other caring adults can give him at this unhappy time. Second, he shares a terrible secret with the molester, who may exploit this and continue to molest him. And third, the child will not get the professional help that he may need. These problems exacerbate the child victim's emotional trauma, which may continue for years. And the molester gets away with it.

So, why don't children tell their parents about molestation? There may be many reasons. A common one is the child's feelings of confusion and guilt. The child may feel somehow responsible for the sexual contact. Maybe the child was too frightened or timid to interfere with the molester and feels he deserves punishment for not following the safety rules. Maybe the molester is someone the child knows or likes, or is a relative or friend of the parents. Maybe the child cooperated with the molester, out of curiosity or fear. Or maybe the molestation was sexual touching that felt pleasurable to the child.

Molesters often threaten their victims to "keep our secret." Common threats to a child victim are: No one will believe you. You wanted me to do this. Your parents will be ashamed of you. They won't love you anymore. It's your fault. You'll be blamed, not me. A molester may even threaten to harm or kill the child or his parents. Although these threats may seem transparent to us, they confuse and frighten child victims—which is exactly what the molester wants.

Teach your child that if something did happen to him—if he

were molested—it would be the molester's fault. It is *never* the child's fault, even if he made a poor decision or deliberately disobeyed limits set by his parents. You would never blame him. You would always support and protect him, no matter what.

These concepts need to be taught to children at all age levels, using appropriate vocabulary and building upon safety rules previously taught. Below are sample conversations for parents to use as guides for talking to their children about these concepts.

Sample conversation with a preschool boy:

Parent: Remember when we talked about the private part of your body?

Child: My penis?

Parent: That's right. Your penis is the private part of your body. No adult should look at or touch your penis.

Child: Except you or Daddy or the doctor.

Parent: Right. Do you remember what you're supposed to do if an adult wants to look at or touch your penis? Or if an adult wants you to look at or touch his penis?

Child: Yell and tell.

Parent: What does that mean?

Child: Yell "Stop it!" Then come and tell you.

Parent: Good for you. That's right. But now I want to talk about something else. What if the adult wouldn't stop when you told him to? What if he looked at or touched your penis? What should you do?

Child: Find you and tell you.

Parent: That's right. Now, whose fault would it be if that happened? If he touched your penis?

Child: It would be his fault because I told him not to.

Parent: Yes. Would it be *your* fault?

Child: No, it wouldn't be my fault. It would be his fault.

Parent: Right. Now, what if something happened and you forgot to tell him to stop? Whose fault would it be if he touched your penis?

Child: I don't know.

Parent: I'll tell you. It would still be *his* fault. It wouldn't be *your* fault, even if you forgot to yell. Do you know why?

Child: No.

Parent: Because what he did is wrong, and he knows it. It's wrong for an adult to look at or touch a child's private parts. All adults know that it's wrong. So it would *always* be *his* fault. It would *never* be *your* fault. And I would never be mad at you even if you forgot the safety rule. O.K.?

Child: O.K.

Parent: I love you very much and I want you to be safe. If someone does something bad to you, you must always tell me. Don't worry that I might be mad at you or think it's your fault. It would *never* be your fault, no matter what. It would always be the adult's fault that he did something bad.

Child: Would you be mad at him?

Parent: Yes. I would always be mad at someone who did something to hurt you.

Child: What would happen to him?

Parent: I don't know. You and I would talk about it. But you wouldn't have to be around him again. The thing I want you to remember is this: If something like that happened, it would never be your fault. You should always tell me right away. I would never be mad at you. O.K.?

Child: O.K.

Sample conversation with a fourth-grade girl:

Parent: Remember when we talked about child molesters?

Child: Yes.

Parent: A child molester is any adult who tries to took at or touch a child's sex organs, or wants the child to look at or touch the adult's sex organs.

Child: I know that.

Parent: And you know what you should do if someone tried to do that to you, right?

Child: Tell them to stop it, and then tell you.

Parent: That's right. We have this rule because I love you very much and I want you to be safe and happy. I don't want anything bad to happen to you, ever. I don't think anything bad will happen, but I want you to know what to do to protect yourself just in case.

Child: I know what to do.

Parent: Good. Now I want to ask you something. What if the molester didn't stop when you told him to? What if you couldn't make him stop and he touched your private parts? What should you do?

Child: Get away from him and tell you right away.

Parent: Right. Now, here's a question. Whose fault would it be if that happened?

Child: It would be the molester's fault.

Parent: That's right. It wouldn't be your fault, would it?

Child: No.

Parent: Let me ask you another question. What if you didn't tell him to stop for some reason? What if you were afraid? Whose fault would it be then?

Child: I think it would still be his fault.

Parent: Good for you. That's right. It would still be his fault even if you didn't follow the rule for some reason. What if the molester was someone you know? What should you do then?

Child: I guess I should still tell you. But I might not want to get someone in trouble.

Parent: You should always tell me, even if the molester is someone you know. And here's another rule: It's *always* the molester's fault, it's *never* the child's fault, no matter what. O.K.?

Child: O.K.

Parent: It's always the molester's fault because the molester has done something wrong to a child, and he or she knows it's wrong. All adults know that it's wrong. If a molester gets in trouble, it's his own fault, not the child's fault.

Child: What would happen to the molester?

Parent: I don't know. That's something you and I would have to talk about. But I would always be there to protect you and take care of you. I love you very much.

Sample conversation with a ninth-grade girl:

Parent: Remember the news story about the girls who were molested by the band teacher?

Child: Yeah. We already talked about it.

Parent: You know what to do if someone approaches you, right? Even if it's someone you know and like?

Child: I know what to do. That would never happen to me.

Parent: Why not?

Child: Because I wouldn't do it. The teacher didn't tie those girls up or anything. They sort of went along with him.

Parent: Why do you think they did that?

Child: I don't know.

Parent: Do you think it's their fault that it happened?

Child: I'm not sure. Maybe a little.

Parent: Here's what I think. What happened is the fault of the band teacher, not the girls. He's the adult. He's a molester and he did something wrong to them. He committed a crime, and he knows it. Maybe the girls could have made better choices, but that doesn't excuse what he did. It's his fault, not theirs. It's always the molester's fault.

Child: O.K.

Parent: I'm serious about this. I know you'll follow the rules we've discussed, and I don't think anything like this would ever happen to you. But if it did, I'd want you to tell me right away. I would never blame you, no matter what. So please don't ever be afraid to talk to me about anything, O.K.? I'll always be on your side. I love you very much.

Child: O.K.

PEOPLE WHO SEEM GOOD CAN SOMETIMES DO BAD THINGS.

To this point, we've stressed that parents should decide which adults will spend time with their children, and they should make sure that these adults are safe. Parents tell children which adults are trusted adults—those the child can go with or turn to if he has a problem. But we know that inevitably children will come into contact with other adults when we aren't around. They will have to make some decisions about these adults, even if their contact with them is fleeting. Of course, in adolescence and the teenage years, children make more and more of their own decisions, whether we are comfortable with this or not.

Children naturally trust adults to protect them and take care of them. Most adults, of course, are worthy of this trust. As parents, we want our children to know that most adults are good people, but not all. We know that child molesters will take advantage of a child's trust and innocence to do him harm.

Some adults do things that frighten or hurt children. Even very young children can recognize an adult who does bad things—steals things or hurts people. But sometimes it's hard to tell the difference between good and bad adults, especially if the adult is a stranger to the child. There are ways of recognizing a friendly adult who might do something wrong to a child, and this is what we need to teach our children.

Parents need to come to terms with the pal-type child molester, an adult the child knows and likes who tries to seduce him. This is a great betrayal of trust and most upsetting for the child. Is this person good or bad? Does he really want to molest the child, or is the child mistaken? This is a situation likely to induce confusion, doubt, and guilt in a child. If the pal molester is someone the parents also know and like, the child's conflicts are even greater.

It's important to remember that even in this situation, the same rules apply. First, be sure you have taken all necessary steps to ascertain that the adults who spend time with your child are safe. But recognize that even when you have done so, there's always the possibility that you are unaware of someone who would molest your child. Be alert to the adult who shows excessive interest in your child, especially if he wants to be alone with the child.

The second line of defense is your child himself. Remember that the children who are most vulnerable to the pal molester's advances are the neediest kids. Make sure your child gets the attention and affection he needs at home, from you.

This is the time to talk to your child about the "good" adult who does something "bad." You must tell him explicitly that even someone he knows and likes, someone who is especially nice to him— someone he thinks is a "good" adult—could do something wrong to him. This might be confusing to him, because he's used to thinking of this person as good, as a friend who likes him. But if this happens, it is still the molester's fault, not the child's fault. And your child must tell you immediately.

So, what should your child do if an adult he likes, such as his coach, asks him to do something he knows is wrong? Basically, it's still the same rule: Say no, then go. And then tell a parent or trusted adult immediately. Tell your child that this rule applies whenever anyone makes him uncomfortable, even if he can't explain why.

But what if the friendly adult has made no explicit overtures to your child? How can your child identify an adult who may molest him? First, your child may have an instinctive feeling of danger or discomfort, the kind of feeling discussed earlier. If he does, he should leave immediately and tell you about it. It doesn't matter whether he can verbalize the reason for the bad feeling or not.

Second, the adult may touch your child in a way that alerts him to danger. This could be a "bad" touch that hurts, or a touch on a child's private parts, even if it seems inadvertent. If your child experiences bad or confusing touches from an adult, he should be on the alert, even if the adult says that he's your child's friend and is especially nice to him. Your child should believe his own feelings, not the adult's words. And he should always trust his own warning instincts. Whenever an adult touches your child in a way that feels bad or is confusing to him, he should tell the person to stop touching him. Then he should leave and tell you about it.

At this point, take a moment to recall the earlier discussion of common tactics used by child molesters. Remember that the "pal" molester relies on his social skills and position of authority to seduce a vulnerable child. He may use attention and "affection" for the child, or prey upon the child's friendly feeling for the molester. He may offer expensive gifts, special favors, or trips in exchange for sexual contact. Or he may exploit the child's natural curiosity about sex by offering pornography and other "grown-up" experiences.

By contrast, the stranger molester is less subtle: His goal is to get a child alone and isolated as quickly as possible. He relies less on social skill and more on his superior physical strength and size. The stranger may ask the child for directions or some kind of help in order to lure the child close enough to grab him. He may threaten him with a weapon. Or he may just pick a child up bodily and take him somewhere.

We have reviewed the Basic Safety Rules for Children and Key Concepts for Prevention designed to help protect your child from the dangers of molesters. Experts have one additional suggestion for parents: behavior rehearsals with your child. These rehearsals are practice sessions which address common scenarios and teach your child specific behaviors to protect himself. Again, this doesn't have to be a frightening experience for your child. Just as children learn how to stay away from traffic when they ride bikes, they can practice simple behaviors to avoid another kind of danger—the child molester. What follows are suggested exercises for some common scenarios which child molesters use.

HELPFUL EXERCISES

Now is the time to educate your child more explicitly about an abductor/molester, an adult who tries to abduct a child and take him somewhere alone. Experts have defined an area of physical danger for the child. They call it the molester's zone of control, the area within which an adult could forcibly abduct a child. This is basically the strike zone within an adult's reach.

Obviously, our children should always stay outside a molester's zone of control. Once a child comes under the control of an abductor/molester, the child will almost certainly be molested, and may even be kidnapped and killed. You probably don't need to put the fear of death in your child, however. Most children are naturally fearful of being separated from their families. The possibility of being abducted or kidnapped is sufficiently frightening without adding the specter of cold-blooded murder.

The zone of control is important where children are physically approached by an adult at the playground, on the sidewalk, at the mall, etc. All children should be taught to recognize and stay out of the zone of control of any adult who is not a trusted adult.

Law enforcement experts recommend that parents teach their child some actions that he can take to help protect himself from an abductor/molester in specific situations. These techniques all follow the same general pattern: A child should ignore any stranger's request for assistance or other overture. He should learn to recognize and avoid the adult's zone of control. If he feels threatened, he should run to a safe place and tell what happened.

Experts advise role playing with children to help them learn to recognize the most common ploys abductors use. Some examples are:

1. The "lost puppy" scenario
2. A driver asking for directions
3. An adult who offers a gift or asks for help in choosing a gift for another child
4. "Would you like to see my—kittens, pony, computer games, swimming pool, new car?" etc.
5. "Would you help me—carry this inside? Get to my car? Find your friend Bobby? Buy new food for my kittens?" etc.
6. The "I'm going to make you a star" routine

Once your child has learned to recognize these common situations, he should know exactly what to do: ignore the adult, get away, and report the incident.

Help your child recognize and understand the abductor's zone of control through demonstration and practice. Have a friend walk up to your child and ask him a question. Then have him take a step forward and reach for your child. Show your child how far away he has to stay to keep himself out of an adult's zone of control. Then show your child how to skirt around the adult and run toward a place of safety if he feels threatened. You can also practice this with your car by pulling up next to your child on the sidewalk.

Remember: The goal is to keep your child out of the adult's zone of control. Law enforcement experts remind us that this advice applies even if the child is threatened with physical violence or a weapon. A child should scream, struggle, and then run to a place of safety.

What if a man forcefully picks up a young child and runs out of the mall with him? What should the child do? Teach your child to scream and yell as loud as he can: "This isn't my daddy!" He should cause maximum commotion, attracting the attention of nearby adults, struggling and fighting to get free.

These are only examples of rehearsing actions and techniques with your child. As you work with your child, you'll devise your own practice scenarios tailored to your child's life. Remember, your goal is not to scare your child, but to make him savvy and street-smart, a difficult target for a predator.

Now let's consider some emergency situations that can ambush parents. The first scenario is this: There's a gruesome abduction-rape-murder of a child in your town or elsewhere, with lots of national publicity. The missing child's picture is everywhere—on TV, in the newspapers, on posters and flyers—along with tearful pleas from the parents. Live television covers the frenzied search for the child, which proves futile. The child's body is found, engendering even more media coverage.

Unless your child is very young, he will almost certainly hear about this even if you don't tell him—and he will be frightened and upset. Recently, a Florida mother told me that her six-year-old son had been sleeping in her bed for months, ever since the abduction of Jimmy Ryce in Florida in September 1995. Even though the killer had been arrested and the case had faded from the news, her child was still too fearful to spend a night in his own bed. What should she tell him? What should she do?

First, remember that these cases of stranger abduction are statistically rare, estimated at about 5 percent of reported missing children. Yet when they occur, these cases play upon every parent's deepest fears. Media coverage is broad and intense as we wait with the terrified parents to learn the fate of the missing child. Even if the child's body is recovered, the story doesn't end. We want a criminal punished. We want justice for the murdered child and solace for the child's family. When there's an arrest and a trial, as happened during the summer of 1996 in the Polly Klaas case in California, there is even more media coverage, replaying the events of the nightmare crime.

Tragedies like the Polly Klaas and Jimmy Ryce abductions provide an opportunity for parents to reinforce lessons previously taught, or to begin an active family plan for child safety if none has yet been established. So when a high-profile crime occurs, the first step is to give your child some appropriate information about the case, *before* he learns about it at school or on TV, if possible. Keeping in mind your child's age and level of knowledge, give him the basic known facts about the incident.

For example, when Jimmy Ryce was first reported missing, a parent might have said something like this: "You may hear about a little boy who is missing. His name is Jimmy Ryce. He was walking home from school and he disappeared. No one knows what happened or where he is, but everyone is trying to find him."

This is a good opportunity to discuss basic child safety strategies, such as the buddy system. You should also remind your child what to do if he is ever confronted by a stranger, as discussed above. Respond to any questions your child may have, in a calm, matter-of-fact way. If your child seems especially fearful, you may want to arrange to pick him up after school for a while. Be sure to spend extra time with him now.

Three months after Jimmy Ryce's disappearance, we learned that he had in fact been abducted by a stranger who threatened him with a gun, and that he had been sodomized and then shot to death. His alleged killer was apprehended and eventually led police to the child's dismembered remains. This was widely reported on TV and in the newspapers. At this point, a parent would have to discuss much more difficult issues with his child. Why did this happen? Did Jimmy do something wrong? Why would a person do something like this? Could this happen to me?

First, parents should remember to stress that the abduction isn't the fault of the child. Even if it turns out that the child didn't make the best decision in the circumstances—didn't follow safety rules, for example, or accepted a ride with a stranger—what happened still isn't the child's fault. The fault is the abductor's. Abduction and molestation are crimes, and the abductor is a criminal.

A more difficult question to address is why someone would do such horrible things to a child. The truth is, even the experts don't really know what makes someone a child molester. Remember to reassure your child that most adults are well-meaning and protective toward children. But even a seemingly "good" adult can do something very wrong. And even a nice, friendly, pleasant adult can be a dangerous person.

A parent could say something like this: "No one knows for sure why some people do bad things to children. This doesn't happen very often. Most adults care for children and try to help them and protect them. But since we know that there are some adults who would do bad things to children, we follow certain rules to keep children safe."

Experts tell us that whenever a child becomes aware of a frightening event like the Jimmy Ryce abduction, the child may regress in his behavior. This is a normal reaction, especially for a young child, and parents should expect that their child may temporarily return to behaviors he exhibited when he was younger: clinging, seeking reassurance and attention, wanting to sleep with the parent, even bed-wetting and thumb sucking. Parents should be tolerant of this temporary regression and provide as much reassurance and attention as their child needs. This is a stressful time, but it will pass and the child will return to more age-appropriate behavior.

During this time, it's especially important to be sensitive to your child's fears and encourage him to discuss them with you. Then you can address any specific situation that is worrying him and discuss how you and your child can work together to keep him safe. Your child may ask directly whether such a thing (what happened to Jimmy Ryce) could happen to him. You want to reassure him that he is safe and that his world is generally a safe place.

A parent might say something like this: "Of course, anything *can* happen, but I don't think this will happen to you." You can then review the safety rules that apply to the situation.

One aspect of the Jimmy Ryce case might be especially upsetting to your Child: The stranger used a gun to force Jimmy into his truck. What should your child do if a stranger makes a physical threat or uses a weapon to try to force him into a car? As discussed earlier, most law enforcement experts say that even in the face of threatened violence, a child should not go with a stranger. What the molester wants is not to kill the child on the spot, but rather to abduct the child and get away. The molester fears getting caught, so anything that calls attention to him in public is bad news for him. Take this opportunity to remind your child that if he is threatened by anyone, he should yell and scream, creating as much noise and commotion as possible—and then run as fast as he can to a place of safety.

Most parents are uncomfortable discussing the specifically sexual aspects of these notorious crimes with their children. In some cases (as with older children), it may be necessary to talk about it; in other cases, it is not necessary. In deciding whether you need to address this with your child, use your common sense and keep in mind your child's age and level of knowledge. In general, younger children may not be aware of any sexual connotations in the event. Most experts advise that parents not introduce this unless the child specifically asks about it. When a child does ask, follow the general rule in answering any question about sex: *Provide only the information that the child seeks.* Be guided by the child's level of sophistication and interest.

What if your child confides a worrisome incident to you? You have laid the foundation for this by teaching your child about his right to bodily privacy, by assuring him that you would never blame him if something bad happened to him, and by promising always to be on his side. Now, how do you handle it if your child comes to you with such a problem?

First, you keep your own emotions under control. Listen to your child and try to stay calm. You want to give him your reassurance, love, and emotional support, without letting your own feelings get in the way. If your child complains to you about someone's conduct, don't jump to the conclusion that he has been sexually attacked. Don't interrogate your child. Let him tell you what is concerning him.

If someone your child knows well has done something that worries or confuses him, find out what has led to his discomfort. How well do you know the person he's complaining about? If you and your child conclude that the episode was not threatening, decide what to do about it. How does your child feel? Would he prefer not to be around this person anymore? Or can he be comfortable again so long as this person follows some behavioral guidelines?

Here's a sample conversation with a kindergarten boy:

Child: There's something I want to talk to you about.
Parent: Sure. What's on your mind?
Child: Something happened at school that I didn't like.
Parent: Tell me about it.
Child: When we came in from the playground, I had to go to the bathroom.
Parent: Yes?
Child: While I was going to the bathroom, Mrs. Smith came in without knocking.
Parent: Mrs. Smith, the teacher's aide?
Child: Yeah. I was going to the bathroom and she saw my penis.
Parent: What happened then?
Child: I told her to go away, that I was going to the bathroom. And I didn't want her to look at my penis.
Parent: Then what happened?
Child: She told me it didn't matter. She has little boys at home and she's seen penises before.

Parent: Then what?

Child: She left.

Parent: How did you feel?

Child: I was mad at her. She wasn't supposed to see my penis. She didn't knock when she came in the bathroom. And she didn't say she was sorry.

Parent: I see. Did you talk to her about it again?

Child: No.

Parent: I think she was wrong to come in the bathroom without knocking. She didn't respect your privacy, did she?

Child: No.

Parent: Were you afraid when she came in the bathroom?

Child: Afraid? No, I was embarrassed. Then I was mad. I did what you told me. I told her to go away and stop looking at me. But she wouldn't do it.

Parent: I'm glad you told her to go away. And I'm glad you told me about it, too. That was the right thing to do. How do you feel now?

Child: I'm not so mad now. But I hope she doesn't do that again.

Parent: I hope she doesn't do that again, too. She shouldn't just walk in like that. She should respect your privacy. Would you like me to talk to her about it?

Child: O.K.

Now what? In the preceding conversation, a parent would want to talk to the adult involved in the incident. In a nonconfrontational way, a parent should make his child's feelings known and show his concern and respect for those feelings. If the parent concludes that the adult's behavior was insensitive rather than threatening, he could work with the adult to establish specific guidelines for the future, and then monitor the situation to be sure there's no further problem.

What if your child tells you about an incident that really worries you? Something that you feel could be an indication of a serious problem with an adult?

Review the following sample conversation with a sixth-grade boy.

> *Parent:* It's time to get ready for your church youth group. Go wash up and get dressed.
>
> *Child:* I don't want to go.
>
> *Parent:* What? Why not?
>
> *Child:* I just don't feel like it.
>
> *Parent:* But you planned to go, and your friends will be there. I'm sure Mr. Wilson will be expecting you. Did something change your mind about going?
>
> *Child:* I just don't want to.
>
> *Parent:* Are you feeling all right?
>
> *Child:* Yeah.
>
> *Parent:* Is something bothering you? You know you can tell me if there's something on your mind.
>
> *Child:* Well, sort of.
>
> *Parent:* O.K.
>
> *Child:* I don't really like Mr. Wilson anymore.
>
> *Parent:* O.K. Why not?
>
> *Child:* I just don't.
>
> *Parent:* Has he been mean to you?
>
> *Child:* Not really.
>
> *Parent:* Has he done something to upset you?
>
> *Child:* I don't know.
>
> *Parent:* How do you feel when you're around him?
>
> *Child:* I don't know. Kind of creepy, sometimes. I can't explain it.
>
> *Parent:* Tell me about the last time you felt creepy around him.
>
> *Child:* At the church picnic. We were all playing and roughhousing and he was tickling me.
>
> *Parent:* Uh-huh.
>
> *Child:* Well, I just didn't like it.
>
> *Parent:* You didn't like the tickling?
>
> *Child:* Right.
>
> *Parent:* How did you feel when he was tickling you?
>
> *Child:* He wouldn't stop when I wanted him to.

Parent: Where was he tickling you?

Child: Just on the ribs. I told him to stop, but he didn't. Then finally he stopped.

Parent: Then what?

Child: He acted like nothing happened. Then he was really, really nice to me. He was hugging me and everything. But I didn't want him to.

Parent: Is this why you don't want to go on the church trip?

Child: Yeah. Do I have to go?

Parent: No, you don't. I'm concerned that Mr. Wilson did that to you. I'm sorry it happened.

Child: He wasn't really hurting me. More like bothering. Besides, I thought you liked Mr. Wilson.

Parent: I did like Mr. Wilson. I thought he was a good person. But I don't like what he did to you.

Child: I don't think I like him anymore.

This situation calls for more concern by the parent. Is Mr. Wilson just socially insensitive or inept, or might this be a warning of a more serious problem? Again, it's important not to jump to conclusions or alarm your child. In the above example, the parent decided not to force the child to go on the outing—an important first step. But what next? There are a number of options for the parent.

Since the situation is ambiguous—the adult has not made any explicit overtures to the child—there are no grounds for making a formal complaint against the adult. The parent could choose simply to withdraw the child permanently from the activity without explanation. Or the parent could request a meeting with Mr. Wilson and the supervisor of the program to discuss the incident. At a meeting, the parent should not make accusations or be confrontational, but rather express concern about the incident and listen to any explanations or suggestions which are offered. Then if the parent is satisfied with the outcome, and the child wants to continue in the activity, the child could return to the group. However, the situation should be closely monitored, perhaps with the parent as a frequent chaperone. If there is any doubt, resolve it in favor of your child's safety. Keep him away from any situation that makes you worry.

But what if your child tells you about an incident that's not ambiguous? What if an adult makes explicit overtures to your child? Or what if—your worst nightmare—you think your child has been molested? These important topics are the subject of the following chapter.

WHAT IF YOU THINK YOUR CHILD HAS BEEN MOLESTED?

Suppose your child wants to talk about something very serious, such as an overt act by an adult. Again, let him tell what happened in his own way. Try not to pry, but let him take his time in getting the story out. Realize that this may take more than one conversation. If he is reluctant to talk, let him know that you'll be there to listen whenever he's ready.

As you listen to your child, you're likely to be frightened, angry, and upset. But for the moment, try to focus on the child's problem rather than your own emotions. Be careful not to react with alarm to what your child says, or vent your anger in a way that seems directed at your child. Don't say, "Why were you there with him in the first place?" If your child has made a bad decision or even disobeyed you, this isn't the time to discuss it. Remember to reinforce that what the molester did is wrong. Never make excuses for the molester. It's his fault, and you won't blame your child no matter what.

Sample conversation with a sixth-grade girl:

Child: I want to talk to you about something.
Parent: You look upset. What's wrong?
Child: My P.E. teacher did something today that I didn't like.
Parent: Oh?
Child: He tried to kiss me. And he tried to touch my chest.
Parent: He did?
Child: He's always asking me to come into his office, by the gym. I don't want to, and sometimes I pretend that I have to see another teacher.
Parent: And what happened today?
Child: Oh, maybe it was nothing. Maybe he just likes me. He always tries to be nice to me.
Parent: How did you feel when he tried to kiss you and touch you?
Child: I felt yucky. I was embarrassed and sort of grossed out.
Parent: Were you scared?
Child: Maybe, a little. I felt confused.
Parent: Honey, I'm so sorry this happened to you. Remember when we talked about good touch and bad touch?
Child: Yeah.
Parent: How do you feel about it now?
Child: Icky. And I don't want to have to see him at school tomorrow.
Parent: I can understand that.
Child: Can I stay home from school tomorrow?
Parent: I don't know right now. I think what your teacher

did was wrong, and I'm very concerned about it.
We need to decide what to do.

Child: Why don't you just let me stay home?

Parent: Well, I—

Child: I knew I shouldn't have told you!

Parent: You did the right thing by telling me. You know I'm
on your side. I love you very much, and I'm here to
protect you. I think your teacher has a problem,
and he needs help. But that's no excuse for what he
did to you. What he did was wrong, and I'm very
concerned about it.

Child: I don't want to talk about this anymore.

Parent: All right. I'm here whenever you're ready to talk,
O.K.? I love you very much, and I'm sorry this happened to you.

What do you do now? This incident is far different from the
ambiguous episodes discussed in the previous chapter. In this example, the teacher's behavior is overt and should be viewed as a warning; and the child clearly feels threatened. What should a parent do
next?

Whenever a parent has reason to suspect that someone may be a
molester, as in this example, the parent should contact the police
immediately and turn the matter over to them. Be prepared to give
as much identifying information as possible about the person you
suspect, and state the reasons you are suspicious. The police are the
ones who can evaluate the appropriate course of action—further investigation, background check, interviews, the possibility of criminal charges, etc.

Law enforcement experts recommend that a parent *not* con-
front the suspected molester directly. Don't undertake your own investigation or make any further allegations. Let the police contact
the school authorities. *Do not* try to take the law into your own
hands. Let the professionals handle it.

In the meantime, a parent would want to keep the child away
from the adult. The child might be permitted to stay home from
school for a day or two while the parent makes arrangements with

the school to put the child in a different class. Should the parent tell the school authorities the reason for the class change? Again, this should be discussed with the police. If an investigation is initiated, the police may request that the parent not discuss the incident with the school authorities or anyone else. If so, a parent could simply insist on the change without explanation, or cite a non-specific "personality conflict."

Suppose the police conclude that there is no basis for further action. Suppose there is no investigation, no charges; the matter is simply dropped. What should a parent do then? With his own child protected from contact with the adult, should the parent just drop it? Or should other parents be warned?

Depending upon how strongly a parent feels about the incident and the adult, the parent might choose to discuss the matter with school authorities. Again, this should be done without accusations or allegations, but rather a simple description of the facts of the incident and the parent's concerns. Discussing the incident with other parents is a more difficult question, but the same principles apply. If a parent feels danger signals, he could describe the incident and his concerns to other parents, avoiding any specific accusations.

Now let's examine another scenario. Suppose a specific incident of child molestation has taken place in your town. Let's use the example of the scout leader discussed earlier, and add that the victims are boys your child knows. The police suspect that the scout leader has molested other children, possibly other boys in the scout troop. The authorities are asking that parents of all children who might have been molested by this man—including all present and former members of his troop—contact them if they believe their child might be a victim. Suppose your child is a member of the troop. How do you find out whether he's been victimized?

When you talk to your child, remember to keep your own emotions under control as much as possible. Your questions should be open-ended, calm, and nonthreatening. Don't put words in your child's mouth or indicate that you expect any particular response from him. And don't repeat allegations of molestation.

Sample conversation with a fifth-grade boy:

Parent: There's something I need to talk to you about. Do you remember when we discussed child molesters?

Child: Yeah.

Parent: I'm glad you remember. When we talked about it, I told you that a child molester is someone who tries to look at or touch a child's private parts, or wants the child to touch the molester's privates.

Child: I know.

Parent: Has anybody ever tried to do this to you?

Child: Huh-uh.

Parent: No?

Child: No.

Parent: You know I want you to tell me right away if someone ever tries to do that to you.

Child: I know.

Parent: I want you to tell me because it's wrong for any adult to do this. It's against the law.

Child: I remember.

Parent: There are other reasons I want you to tell me right away. One is because I think it would be very upsetting for you, and I'd want you to talk with me about it. O.K.?

Child: O.K.

Parent: If you couldn't talk with me about it for some reason, I'd want you to talk to someone else that you trust. Maybe Dad or your teacher or your counselor at school. Just as long as you talked to some adult right away.

Child: I would.

Parent: Good. You know I never want you to be around anyone who might do something to hurt you. That's another reason I'd want you to tell me right away. If there was someone like that around you— at school or wherever—I would want to know right away. A person like that shouldn't be around children at all. Right?

Child: Right.

Parent: I'm glad we talked about this. I want you to keep this in mind, and if there's anything you want to talk to me about, I'm always ready to listen. O.K.?

Child: O.K.

Remember that children are often reluctant to admit that they have been molested for a variety of reasons: threats from the molester, guilt, shame, fear of punishment, even affection for the molester. We know that children who have been sexually molested may deny outright that there's been any such activity, or they may be merely evasive. This is where your knowledge of your own child is crucial. If your child tells you that there's been no such activity and you believe him, let it drop. As in the sample conversation above, tell him to keep this in mind, and if there's anything he wants to talk to you about, you'll listen any time.

What should you do if you believe that your child has actually been molested? First, try to get your own emotions under control. You're likely to be filled with rage at the molester. You may also be feeling some guilt that you weren't able to protect your child from this. You may decide to get professional help for your family in dealing with this crisis. But first, what should you do for your child?

Start by being compassionate and supportive. Tell your child that you love him very much and that you'll always love him, no matter what. If someone has done something wrong to him, it's not his fault. Remind him that there should be no secrets kept from you. It's not wrong "to tell on" an adult, even (or *especially*) when the adult has asked the child to keep "their secret." It's wrong *not* to tell the truth to parents. There may be things your child is uncomfortable discussing with you. You might be uncomfortable, too, but that's all right. It's important to talk about these things even if everyone is uncomfortable.

Experts say that interviewing child victims of sexual molestation demands sophisticated professional training. They remind us that most child victims initially deny that they've been molested.

Disclosure of molestation is a process that may take considerable time as the child victim moves from denial to tentative disclosure, and finally to active disclosure. For these reasons, most experts recommend that a specially trained professional should be the one to interview a possible child victim of sexual molestation.

However, if you believe that your child has been sexually molested, you have an immediate and imperative goal: You need to know enough about what has happened so that you can decide whether this is a medical emergency for your child. In this situation, you're not trying to interrogate your child or act like a professional investigator. You're just trying to get some basic information to help your child in what may be a medical crisis for him.

In a nonthreatening manner, find out what the molester did. Did he look at or fondle the child's sex organs in a nonviolent way? Or did he cause pain, physical injury, or penetration? If the child suffered pain, physical injury, or penetration, this is an emergency and you should seek medical help immediately.

Call your child's doctor and take him for an examination. There may be some infection or injury that requires treatment, or there may be physical evidence of molestation. But remember that the absence of physical evidence doesn't mean there has been no molestation. You should prepare your child for this examination by telling him that the doctor needs to examine him to be sure he's all right. The same-sex parent should stay with the child during the examination. If your child's doctor is not available, take him to a hospital emergency room.

Call the police. They will assign an investigator to the case, probably an officer of the sex crimes unit or crimes-against-children unit of your local police department. Sometimes a specially trained psychologist or counselor will be available to interview child victims or to work with parents. If professional help is available, use it.

Consider counseling for your child and your family. Ask a law enforcement professional or your child's pediatrician for a referral to someone specially trained in working with child victims and their families. This is an extremely stressful situation for the entire family. Experts emphasize that therapy and support for the victim and his family help reduce trauma and improve the child's recovery rate.

In the meantime, offer emotional support and comfort to your child. If he wants to talk about what happened to him, listen, but don't interrogate him. Reassure him that this wasn't his fault, that you don't think it will happen again, and that he's surrounded now by people who love him and will protect him.

The steps to take are summarized in the checklist below. This list is repeated in the Appendix.

WHAT TO DO IF YOU BELIEVE THAT YOUR CHILD HAS BEEN MOLESTED

EMERGENCY CHECKLIST:

1. Keep your own emotions under control.

2. Be supportive and reassuring to your child.

3. If you believe your child may have suffered pain, physical injury, or penetration, take him to the doctor or emergency room.

4. Call the police. Be prepared to explain why you think your child has been molested and whom you suspect.

5. Obtain therapy by a trained professional for your child and your family.

Sometimes children who have been sexually molested continue to deny to parents that anything has happened to them. Some children will confide in a sibling or playmate who then tells the parents. There are also certain behavioral clues that may alert parents to the possibility of molestation. Basically, these clues amount to a significant, persistent, and negative change in your child's behavior, especially aggressive behavior or sexually overt acting out.

BEHAVIORAL CLUES

1. Change in disposition; a happy, well-behaved child becoming aggressive or withdrawn

2. Sexualized behavior, sexual acting out, or inappropriate statements with sexual content

3. Sleep disturbances, including nightmares

4. Problems in school, either behavioral or academic

5. Reluctance to engage in activities the child formerly enjoyed, or to play with friends he used to like

6. Avoidance of a particular adult that the child used to spend time with

7. Weight loss or decrease in appetite

8. Listlessness, feelings of sadness or depression

9. Complaints of illness or physical symptoms

Of course, such changes don't necessarily indicate that a child is concealing sexual molestation. But you should be alert to such symptoms if they persist over a substantial period of time. Consider taking your child to a trained psychologist, therapist, or counselor who can evaluate the reasons for these changes.

There has been much attention recently to the problem of false allegations of child sexual abuse. Experts tell us that very few children make up allegations of sexual abuse out of whole cloth. The problem of false allegations is usually caused by parents or other adults who transmit their fears and ideas to children. For example, in a bitter divorce case where child custody is an issue, there may be allegations of child sexual abuse by one parent against the other that turn out to be false. Experts say that the source of these false allegations is usually the adult, not the child. Sometimes a parent will unconsciously put words in a child's mouth, or a child may sense what his parent wants to hear. This is one more reason experts recommend that where there are allegations of child sexual abuse, trained professionals should take charge.

When a child has been molested and the molester has been arrested and charged, his parents face a very difficult decision: whether, and to what extent, their child should participate in the criminal justice system. First there will be interviews: with the police and prosecutors, and perhaps with the state's psychologist. A goal of enlightened law enforcement is to minimize the number of interviews with the child victim of sexual molestation. The more interviews a child has to endure, the greater the likelihood of additional emotional trauma to him. There's also an increased risk that the child may recant his testimony in order to escape the emotional stress of the situation, perhaps jeopardizing the prosecution's case against the molester.

If the molester does not enter into a plea agreement and the state decides to take the case to trial, the child may be asked to testify at trial. In deciding whether their child should testify, parents have to consider many factors: the child's age, his willingness to testify, and his level of sophistication; his adjustment and progress in therapy; the advice of the counselor or therapist; and the parents' own ability to cope with the situation. Parents will also want to know whether their state has laws permitting child victims to testify by videotape or closed-circuit TV from a room outside the courtroom, and keeping the identity of the child victim confidential. These laws are a positive step in getting molesters convicted while protecting the child victims as much as possible. Needless to say, having a young child testify in open court against a molester—and subjecting him to a defense attorney's cross-examination—can be extremely traumatic. Some states provide trained victim advocates to work with a child victim and his family. If this assistance is available, parents should use it.

WHEN A CHILD IS MISSING

What could be worse than sexual molestation of your child? Only one thing: having your child disappear. In the worst nightmare scenario, your child fails to come home from school.

You wait a half hour, then go looking for him. You go to the school, checking with the teacher and principal, who tell you that he left at the usual time and they haven't seen him since then. You go back home, call all his friends and their parents. No luck. You check every place he could possibly be—including sleeping in his own room. You go through the neighborhood, all the special places he likes to play, but there's no sign of him. Now you're really scared. More than three hours have passed. What do you do?

When Claudine and Don Ryce discovered that their son, Jimmy, was missing, they were confused and frightened. Claudine and Don, both attorneys, are devoted parents in addition to being sophisticated, well-educated professionals. Like most of us, they never dreamed this could happen to their adored child. As hours passed, then days, weeks, and finally months, they did everything they could think of to bring their son back. Although they were unable to save him, what the Ryces did serves as an excellent model for any other family unfortunate enough to have a child missing. Here's what the Ryces did and what they learned along the way:

First, of course, they eliminated all the innocent possibilities of their son's whereabouts—staying after school, visiting a friend, playing in the neighborhood, etc. Once they knew Jimmy was really missing, they called the police. They gave the authorities an excellent physical description of their son and a recent photograph: the touching picture that became so familiar, a sweet faced boy with a toothy grin, wearing a baseball cap. They provided details about the clothes and backpack he was wearing when he disappeared. They also gave the photograph, physical description, and circumstances of Jimmy's disappearance to the news media. Within hours, Jimmy's photograph was on the local TV news. The next morning, it was in the *Miami Herald.*

Don Ryce candidly states that he and his wife were the initial suspects in their son's disappearance. He explains that the parents are always the logical first step in such an investigation; they must be cleared—that is, eliminated as suspects—as quickly as possible so that police can focus their energies in the right direction. The parents' first task, then, is to establish trust and a working partnership with law enforcement officers. Don Ryce urges parents to cooperate with police and do whatever is necessary to help them move the investigation along. In this case, the Ryces were eager to take polygraph tests (which they passed) to establish their innocence, so that the search for Jimmy could proceed.

Several law enforcement agencies devoted countless man-hours to the search for Jimmy Ryce. First on the scene were local police detectives from the Metro-Dade Police Department. Then the statewide agency, the Florida Department of Law Enforcement (FDLE), extended the search across Florida, and the FBI expanded the search to the national level.

While the law enforcement professionals organized their search, the Ryces enlisted their friends, colleagues, neighbors, and family. Some were assigned to man a phone line at the Ryce home, taking calls from anyone who might have information about Jimmy. Others canvassed the neighborhood door-to-door. The Ryces printed up thousands of posters with Jimmy's picture almost overnight, and teams of volunteers pasted them up all over town: in stores, restaurants, shopping malls, schools, banks, gas stations, etc. A fax line was set up in the Ryce home. They faxed copies of the poster all over the country, to media outlets, law enforcement agencies, anywhere they could think of. Volunteers manned the phone and fax lines twenty-four hours a day for three months. The printing and long-distance telephone calls alone were a significant financial burden, one that the family is still dealing with.

Don and Claudine Ryce realized that with the passing of time, their son could be anywhere in the country—indeed, anywhere in the world. They wanted to put flyers in federal government buildings across the nation, but they were told this was "not authorized." In one instance, they discovered that an expensive, full-color flyer sent to a U.S. post office had been thrown in the trash. Don Ryce was furious. Why, he asked, is it O.K. to put a poster of the ten most wanted criminals in the post office but not a poster of a missing child? At the Ryces' urging, President Clinton later signed an executive order authorizing the Government Services Administration to post flyers of missing children in federal buildings.

The Ryces contacted the professional organization whose special mission is assisting in the search for missing children: The National Center for Missing and Exploited Children (NCMEC), a private, nonprofit organization that works in cooperation with the Office of Juvenile Justice and Delinquency Prevention within the U.S. Department of Justice. Among its many valuable services, the NCMEC operates a twenty-four-hour toll-free hotline for reporting missing children (1-800-THE-LOST).

As soon as it receives information about a missing child, the NCMEC disseminates child photographs and descriptions, and breaking case information, to all law enforcement and news media in targeted areas through its Missing Child Alert program. Since its inception in 1984, the NCMEC has handled nearly one million calls to its hotline. Out of the nearly 40,000 missing-child cases on which the NCMEC has worked with law enforcement, more than 25,000 children were recovered.

Nancy McBride, director of the Florida Branch of the NCMEC, performed an especially valuable service for the Ryces by putting them in touch with Patrick Sessions in Miami. Sessions is the father of Tiffany Sessions, a University of Florida student who disappeared while jogging near her apartment in Gainesville, Florida. Her disappearance remains unsolved. Patrick Sessions is an activist for missing children, and he has been affiliated with the Adam Walsh Foundation and the NCMEC. But according to Don Ryce, Session's most valuable role is that of friend and counselor to other parents of missing children. He's been there. They know it, and they trust him. Sessions gave Don and Claudine valuable advice at a time when they desperately needed it. Be careful of your health, he reminded them. Don't forget to eat once in a while and try to get some rest. And don't forget about Jimmy's siblings. They are suffering as much as you are, even though they're trying to be strong for you. Patrick Sessions was a source of great comfort for the family.

Claudine and Don Ryce decided to set up a reward for information leading to Jimmy's safe return. They contacted an attorney friend, Craig Stein, who handled the legal details for them pro bono. They had reward posters and flyers printed and disseminated throughout the country.

The Ryces and their friends kept working, contacting everyone they knew who might be in a position to help: prosecutors, cops, politicians, local commissioners, the mayor, all the way up to Janet Reno, attorney general of the United States and a Miami native. While it's true that Claudine and Don Ryce are highly regarded, well-connected attorneys, it's also true that "everybody knows somebody." This is the time to pull out all the stops, to call in all your chits, to mine all your contacts. There will never be a more important cause than this.

The Ryces mobilized the entire community, indeed all of South Florida, in the search for Jimmy. For three months after his disappearance, Jimmy's parents devoted every waking moment to finding him. Neither parent was able to work, and their family income plummeted. They appeared on every national TV program that would have them, including Oprah Winfrey's show, which is always sympathetic to children's issues.

In fact, the day after Claudine and Don appeared on *Oprah*, the police called to say that they had arrested a suspect in the case—a local handyman, someone the Ryces had never heard of, who lived in their neighborhood. The next few days of waiting for more information about Jimmy—waiting to learn whether he was dead or alive—were "pure hell," says Don Ryce. The Ryces prayed for a miracle, but tried to prepare themselves for the worst.

The clue that unraveled the mystery of Jimmy's disappearance was heartbreaking. A neighbor, who didn't know the family personally, spotted a child's backpack and a flyer about Jimmy's disappearance in a suspicious location: the house trailer that her temporary handyman was living in. The neighbor didn't immediately realize the significance of what she had found. But her son recognized Jimmy's picture from the barrage of publicity about him and suspected that the backpack was Jimmy's. He called police and the handyman was arrested. The suspect confessed to the murder a few days later, and then led police to the child's remains.

Don Ryce is firmly convinced that ongoing publicity was crucial in solving his son's disappearance and arresting his killer. Even though they couldn't save their son, the Ryces remain committed to helping other families with missing children. They have established the Jimmy Ryce Center for Victims of Predatory Abduction (see Appendix), which offers assistance to families in any abduction where there is reason to believe that a child is in imminent physical danger. In addition to immediate help for families, the Center provides education, assistance, and advice regarding any issue related to predatory abductions. They have established a toll-free hotline for parents to use: 1-800-JIM-RYCE.

The steps to take are summarized in the checklist below. This list is repeated in the Appendix.

WHAT TO DO IF YOUR CHILD IS MISSING

EMERGENCY CHECKLIST:

1. Call the police. Be prepared to give a physical description of your child and the clothes he was wearing, his last known whereabouts, and a recent photograph.

2. Cooperate with the police to get yourself cleared as a suspect as quickly as possible so that search efforts can be properly directed. Establish a relationship of trust and cooperation with the police and let them do their job.

3. Call local news media and provide appropriate information and photographs. Establish and maintain a partnership with news media to promote ongoing publicity about your missing child.

4. Call the NCMEC (1-800-THE-LOST) and provide all relevant information, photographs, etc.

5. Call the Jimmy Ryce Center (1-800-JIM-RYCE) for assistance.

6. Arrange for someone to monitor your home telephone at all times.

7. Organize your friends, relatives, colleagues, and neighbors to help with the search.

8. Use your contacts and friends-of-friends to get assistance in your search and publicity efforts.

9. Prepare flyers and posters with your child's picture and relevant information. Distribute these to police, the news media, and throughout the community—to stores and restaurants, shopping malls, public buildings, gas stations, schools, everywhere you can think of.

10. Consider offering a reward for information about your child. Contact an attorney to help you with the details.

LEGISLATION, AND WHAT YOU CAN DO TO HELP

Consider these news reports:

• In New Jersey, a young girl named Megan Kanka was abducted, raped, and murdered, allegedly by a man who had been previously convicted—twice—of sexual molestation. This convicted molester had served a prison sentence, and then was released into the unsuspecting community where Megan lived.

• In Fort Lauderdale, Florida, furious parents picketed local authorities about a convicted child molester who moved into a house across the street from an elementary school. Another child molester arrested in the area was carrying a list of public schools that he had torn from the telephone book.

• In Miami, a popular school band director was accused of sexually molesting some of his students. One young girl committed suicide, allegedly over the end of their "affair." In the ensuing investigation, it was learned that the band director had similar "problems" in his previous position at a school in another state. To get rid of him, those school authorities agreed to let him resign rather than be fired; and they gave him a "highest recommendations" employment reference so that he could get another job somewhere else. When Miami officials checked the director's references before they hired him, they were told in writing: "An exceptional teacher, you won't be sorry if you hire [him]." They weren't told anything about his previous "problems."

These events highlight problems that hamper prevention efforts and law enforcement in child sexual molestation cases. And they require us to reexamine our philosophy about crime and punishment as it applies to child molesters. If there is no "cure" for habitual child molesters—and, worse, no "cure" for their child victims—should they *ever* be released back into society? Can these criminals ever "pay their debt to society," as we think of it in connection with other crimes? If they are never to be released, what should happen to them? Conversely, if they should be eligible for release, when, where, and under what conditions? And, most important, how can their potential child victims be protected from them? These questions raise an even more fundamental issue: How can we balance our societal commitment to individual freedom as embodied in the Bill of Rights against the rights of innocent child victims of sexual molestation? This same issue underlies the public's frustration over the state of our criminal justice system in general, and the widely held belief that the system unfairly protects criminals' rights at the expense of the rights of their innocent victims.

These are troubling questions that state and federal lawmakers are beginning to address in the context of child sexual molestation.

The manner in which legislation answers these questions will have a profound impact on the success or failure of prevention efforts and law enforcement in child sexual molestation cases—and a profound impact on the safety and security of all our children.

All citizens, and especially parents, have a tremendous stake in the outcome of this process. It's up to us to work together for changes to ensure the safe future of our children and our society.

One piece of federal legislation regarding these issues is particularly important, unique, and far-reaching: The Missing Children's Assistance Act, and the establishment of the National Center for Missing and Exploited Children (NCMEC). This seminal legislation marks the beginning of a national awakening to the epidemic of child abduction, molestation, and sexual exploitation sweeping our society.

In announcing the creation of the NCMEC in 1984, President Ronald Reagan quoted Helen Kromer:

One man awake can 'waken another.
The second can awaken his next door brother.
The three awake can rouse the town
by turning the whole place upside down.
And the many awake make such a fuss,
they finally awaken the rest of us.

The special mission of the NCMEC is to act as a clearinghouse for information regarding missing children, to assist in the search for missing children, and to prevent child victimization. Included within its jurisdiction are cases of child sexual abuse and child abduction by a family member. Perhaps most important, this landmark legislation constitutes a national commitment to the safety and security of our country's children. The NCMEC is headquartered in Arlington, Virginia, with regional branches in New York, California, South Carolina, and Florida (see Resources for phone numbers).

After ten years in operation, the NCMEC prepared a "Report Card to the Nation 1984–1994," which describes and evaluates its services. The "Report Card" also rated the country as a whole and state-by-state on various agenda items. According to the "Report Card," by 1994 we as a nation had become more aware that large numbers of children have been sexually molested (or are at risk for molestation), earning a grade of B-; but our prevention strategy for protecting our children rated only a D+. A new report card is planned for release in 1997.

WHAT WE NEED

Effective, far-reaching federal legislation has been implemented to address the problems of missing and sexually exploited children at the national level. But for most of these crimes, law enforcement begins at the local and state level, not the federal level. And state laws vary widely in addressing these problems. What we need is effective laws for states to use in locating missing children, preventing child victimization, and dealing with child predators. And then we need to be sure these laws are strongly enforced.

As part of its mission, the NCMEC has prepared and assembled model state legislation dealing with all aspects of child protection. This model legislation is collected in a publication entitled *Selected State Legislation: A Guidebook for Effective State Laws to Protect Children,* available free from the NCMEC by calling the hotline at 1-800-THE-LOST. This legislation provides an important framework within which to evaluate state laws.

Of particular concern to parents are the NCMEC's model state laws addressing four general areas:

1. Mandatory prison terms for sex offenders and conditions for release

2. Registration of convicted sex offenders and community notification

3. Rights of child victims

4. Prevention of child victimization

Parents should have input with their state legislatures regarding these crucial child protection issues. Later in this chapter, we'll discuss how to make your voice heard, and how you can help ensure that your state has appropriate legislation addressing your concerns.

With regard to the first issue above, appropriate punishment for offenders lies at the heart of a dilemma concerning child molesters. Who should be punished, and how? For how long? And if child molesters are released, how can we be sure they won't do it again? How can we protect our children?

John Sullivan phrases it as a philosophical question: If there is no cure for child molesters, and there's no cure for their victims, should molesters *ever* be released into society? After a thirty-year career in law enforcement, Sullivan answers with a resounding, "No!" In his view, serial child molesters should always be incarcerated—either in prison or in a secure mental health treatment facility. According to Sullivan, it's a near certainty that serial child molesters will repeat their crimes with new child victims as soon as they're released. It's a sham to talk about "paying a debt to society," he says, because this is a debt that can never be paid.

Dr. Jon Shaw, director of child and adolescent psychiatry at the University of Miami School of Medicine, puts it another way: "As long as they're incarcerated, they're safe and the world's safe."

Indeed, Sullivan questions whether capital punishment should be considered for some acts of child molestation. In fact, some states do provide for capital punishment of child molesters under some circumstances. However, as a matter of federal constitutional law, the death penalty may be imposed only for the killing of the victim.

The NCMEC model state legislation demonstrates a moderate view of the subject. This legislation does not contain a capital punishment provision, but it does provide a prison term for anyone convicted of: committing a sexual offense on a minor that results in death or serious bodily injury; or committing a second offense on a minor; or possessing or trafficking in child pornography. The NCMEC legislation permits the judge to make exceptions in sentencing for specified reasons.

Similar issues are raised after a term of incarceration when a convicted sex offender is paroled or released back into the community.

The central question for parents is the safety of potential victims—our children. Will the offender do it again? What's the degree of risk to the community's children? Experts say there is no clear answer because there are so many variables among types of offenders and degrees of offense. A further problem is that mental health and law enforcement professionals are not in agreement about an important underlying issue: what constitutes effective treatment for serial child molesters. Certainly there are a number of therapeutic approaches under active study and trial, but experts speak in terms of treatment, rehabilitation, and containment rather than a cure. And a significant problem previously discussed is that most serial child molesters don't *want* treatment. Unless their active participation in a treatment program is required and closely monitored, they tend to drop out of treatment soon after release.

A second major area of interest to parents is registration of convicted sex offenders and community notification. Recall the story of Megan Kanka, the New Jersey child described above, who was abducted, raped, and murdered, allegedly by a twice-convicted sex offender. In response to that tragedy, the outraged citizens of New Jersey demanded and got a state law requiring that the community be notified whenever a convicted sex offender is released in their area. Known as "Megan's Law," this legislation implicitly recognizes that convicted sex offenders are stripped of certain rights by their convictions, and that the community has an interest in knowing of a sex offender in its midst, especially a child molester. But there has been at least one reported incident of "vigilante justice" in which an innocent man was attacked and beaten because he was mistakenly believed to be a child molester. This has led to criticism of this type of law as encouraging a "shoot first" mentality.

Many states have already passed some version of Megan's Law. Florida has recently adopted a stringent version as part of the Jimmy Ryce Act dealing with sexual predators. Under Florida's law, upon release, the convicted sex offender is required to register his address with the Florida Department of Law Enforcement (FDLE). If, after a hearing, a judge determines that the offender is a "sexual predator" as defined by the statute, the FDLE then notifies the community where the offender resides. Thereafter, the local governing body of the community *must* take out an advertisement in a newspaper once a week for two consecutive weeks that features the offender's photograph, states his criminal conviction, and identifies the general area where the offender lives (without giving the specific address). The ad must also carry a warning that anyone contemplating a reprisal against the offender will face criminal prosecution. This Florida law has only recently taken effect.

It is too soon to tell whether such offender registration and community notification laws will be an effective prevention strategy or a deterrent to serial sexual predators. But there are already indications that they are not a panacea. One recent Florida tragedy has gained national attention as a symbol of society's failure to protect its children from such serial predators: In November of 1996, two little girls were abducted in Fort Lauderdale by a man who had befriended a single-parent family. One child was sexually assaulted; both were murdered. The alleged perpetrator: an unemployed house painter with a long record of sexual assaults on children. He was on probation at the time of the murders, and in fact, his probation officer made a routine visit to his home that same day—shortly after the girls had been abducted. Police later speculated that he had already murdered the children and stashed their bodies in his own attic, where they were later found. Yet the offender behaved "normally" when his probation officer came to visit his home, even though the bodies of the murdered children may have only been several feet overhead in his attic. The probation officer noticed nothing amiss.

This man was on the Florida registry for sexual offenders. His identity was known to the police and available to the community. In fact, in August, 1996, his name and address appeared on the front page of *The Broward County Crusader*, a community newspaper. The headline: "Exclusive! Broward Convicted Sex Offenders."

Responding to this tragedy, one citizen commented, "We are the people. We make the laws. One (offense) and they never see the light of day again."

Another important area of concern for parents is the rights of child victims. As discussed earlier, parents face a particularly difficult situation when their child is asked to participate in criminal proceedings against the molester. The NCMEC model state legislation provides an excellent outline of procedures to minimize the ordeal for the child victim. This legislation provides (among other things) for the following:

1. The appointment of a guardian ad litem or court-appointed special advocate for any child victim. Guardians ad litem and court-appointed special advocates act as advocates for child victims to ensure that their best interests are protected in judicial proceedings

2. A reasonable limitation on the number of interviews of a child victim

3. Protection of the identity of the child victim

4. Authorization for a judge to close a courtroom and remove spectators if he or she finds it necessary to accommodate the child witness

5. Allowing child victims to testify by videotape or closed-circuit television rather than in open court.

The reason for these humane measures is obvious: to protect the child victim from further trauma. There is another objective, and that is to permit and encourage child victims to participate in the criminal proceedings if that is necessary to get the molester convicted. Fortunately, more states are implementing similar legislation.

Finally, and perhaps most important, we return to the subject with which we started: the prevention of child sexual molestation. Of course, child protection is the ultimate goal of all the measures we've discussed. But the NCMEC model state legislation addresses some additional issues that deserve parents' consideration.

We have discussed at length the importance of proper background checks for everyone who comes into contact with children. We know that child molesters often deliberately seek employment or volunteer work that places them in contact with children, in a position of authority and respect. We want to have an effective screening process in place to locate and eradicate molesters from such positions;

and we also want to deter them from even applying for these jobs.

The NCMEC model state legislation provides for screening of all persons providing services to children. This screening includes child abuse registries and federal criminal history checks with fingerprints through the FBI, including the National Crime Information Center Interstate Identification Index, which records criminal history in all states. Conviction of certain crimes would bar an applicant for any position in contact with children, and records of arrests that did not result in convictions could also be obtained.

A related area is the murky ground between *suspicion* of child molestation and arrest or conviction. Recall the Miami school band director accused of sexually molesting his students, one of whom committed suicide. This man previously had similar "problems" at a school in another state, but was permitted by that employer to resign with a "highest recommendations" job reference. When he applied to the Miami school, officials checked with his prior employer, but they were not told about his previous "problems." The result was disastrous. How can we avoid this situation?

Many states have laws that provide some immunity for certain employers who give recommendations regarding a former employee. Greatly simplified, these laws provide that so long as what the employer discloses about the former employee is based upon good faith and reasonable grounds, he is protected from liability if the former employee sues him for libel. This type of law is crucial in all areas where an employee has contact with children.

In the example cited above, the first employer should be in a position to give accurate information about the band director's "problems" at the school without fearing that the band director will get a libel judgment against him. Because there was no arrest or formal legal complaint against the band director, the employer's statement would have to be carefully limited to the established facts without embellishment. The employer could not say, for example, that the band director was a child molester. But he should be allowed to describe the band director's "problems" at the school, whatever inquiry the school undertook, and the outcome of that process. That should give a careful prospective employer sufficient information to determine that this man had no business working with young girls.

Perhaps the most crucial component of the prevention effort is education. The NCMEC advocates education and training about child victimization issues for law enforcement, social service, and judicial personnel, and virtually all professionals who work with children.

Equally important, the NCMEC is committed to personal safety education and training for children and their parents. The NCMEC has developed an excellent program for children in kindergarten through sixth grade, "KIDS AND COMPANY: Together for Safety." This program stresses partnership and communication between parents and school, and provides materials for parents to use for safety discussions with their children at home.

WHAT YOU CAN DO

We must recognize that public education is the key to positive change for children. If you doubt the power of public education to effect social and legal change, think back a moment. Not so long ago, people smoked cigarettes wherever they pleased, drunk driving was tolerated with a wink and a nod, and domestic violence was considered a private family matter rather than a law enforcement concern. Our parents fed us red meat, eggs, butter, and whole milk, and told us to clean up our plates.

Organizations such as MADD—Mothers Against Drunk Driving—demonstrate what committed parents can do to protect their children from drunk drivers. Now it's time for us to work together to protect our children from the sexual predators who stalk them. What will it take to change public attitudes and awareness of this problem? According to John Sullivan, what's required is nothing short of a total blitz: saturation publicity in the news media; education and prevention programs in all our schools; training and multidisciplinary teams in social service agencies, law enforcement, and the legal system; and commitment at every level of government, local, state, and federal. And most important, the dedication of every parent to doing whatever it takes to keep every child safe.

What can you do? If you are a parent of a minor child, your first duty is to your own child. Make sure your child is as safe and street-smart as possible, using the suggestions outlined in this book as a guide.

Whether you are a parent or not, this endeavor needs as much time, energy, and effort as you can give. You now know more than most people about the issues in child sexual molestation and child protection, and how they should be addressed. Start now by thinking over what you've learned. Which areas concern you the most? Which interest you most? Safety education for parents and children in your community? Working for legislative change in your state? Volunteering your time and talents as a victim advocate in your judicial system? Working with child victims and their families?

Next, ask yourself what skills you have to offer. Maybe you're good at organizing groups of volunteers. Maybe you have contacts for lobbying legislators or raising funds. Perhaps you're effective in working with small groups of parents and children, or making presentations to groups like your local school board or the P.T.A. Are you licensed in mental health, law enforcement, or teaching? Whatever your skills and talents—even if you don't think you have anything to offer but interest—there's an important role for you to play.

Now find out what your community and your state really need. You know that state law is the starting point for addressing child protection and criminal justice issues. Find out how your state stacks up in these areas. How can you do that? It's simple—the NCMEC has already done it for you. Call the NCMEC hotline at 1-800-THE-LOST and ask for publications such as the "Report Card to the Nation 1984–1994," which reviews each state's laws with regard to these issues. You may also want a copy of *Selected State Legislation: A Guide for Effective State Laws to Protect Children.* This publication contains all the model state legislation discussed above, together with charts rating each state on every issue and citing specific state statute numbers so that you can find them. This material is clear, concise, and easily understandable. You don't have to be a lawyer to read these publications.

Once you've decided what your state and community need most, you can plan to help. First, canvass your community or state to find out what others are doing. Are there any parent groups or organizations already working on these problems? Check your local school, your school board, your local police department, your town council or commission, social service agencies, your hospitals, your church or temple, your local library, your United Way or other charitable institutions. Is there a college or university nearby? Check their bulletin boards and appropriate departments of study. Call your state representatives and senators. Are there any study committees or citizen groups you can join? Any task forces addressing these issues?

If you conclude that your state laws are adequate, remember that even when strong laws are in place, they need to be strongly enforced. One area you might consider is volunteering as a victim advocate, or monitoring your judicial system's handling of these cases. Some criminal justice experts, including some judges, feel that too many cases of child molestation are plea-bargained down to unacceptable levels. This permits the molester to "get away with it," and return to the community to victimize other children without sufficient jail time or treatment. Of course, some cases don't go to trial because they're not solid, "winnable" cases, and a plea to a reduced charge may be the best that the prosecutor can do. And prosecutors, public defenders, and judges have heavy caseloads that must be accommodated somehow.

But organizations like MADD and advocates for victims of domestic violence have faced these problems and achieved impressive change even in the face of these obstacles. They've accomplished their goals through concerted, committed efforts to educate the public, parents, legislators, and professionals, and to change public attitudes. They've monitored cases through the judicial system, called attention to enforcement problems, publicized the issues relentlessly. And we are all the better for their efforts.

Like these activists, we need to work to ensure that everyone—the public, police, prosecutors, judges, parents, educators—takes these crimes against children seriously. We want enforcement of these laws to be a high priority, so that the temptation to plead them out for short sentences will be avoided. We want the public to demand that these crimes be treated as important matters of public safety, not unmentionable "family" matters to be swept under the rug.

In this regard, another factor deserves mention. Some prosecutors, like some police officers, find this work particularly burdensome and troubling when they don't get the respect and support of their colleagues. Again, this is simply a reflection of our societal attitude toward child sexual molestation: denial. We must recognize and acknowledge that this is important work that should be respected, appreciated, and supported.

We've come full circle, back to the most crucial prevention work: teaching parents and children how to be safe. Your local schools, your police department, social service agencies, mental health clinics, hospitals, libraries—any gathering of people in your community—can sponsor a personal safety program for children and their parents. And you can help—if you're willing.

The second chapter began with a description of John Sullivan's opening remarks in a training session with parents. It's appropriate to close the way he concludes his session:

Would you incur a risk to protect your child? he asks the parents. If so, raise your hand.

(Every hand in the crowded room goes up.)

Let me ask you parents another question, he continues. How many of you are willing to get involved at some level in this effort to protect our children? Raise your hand.

(He waits to see how many hands are raised. Sometimes there are just a few.)

Why is there such a disparity? he asks them. What about those of you who raised your hands the first time? Why won't you get involved? Is it because you don't want to incur the risk? he asks. Is it because you don't have time?

(There are uncomfortable glances around the room.)

Let's try it again, he says.

(This time more hands go up.)

So, how many of you are willing to get involved in this effort to protect our children? Let's see those hands.

APPENDIX

WHAT TO DO IF YOU BELIEVE THAT YOUR CHILD HAS BEEN MOLESTED

EMERGENCY CHECKLIST:

1. Keep your own emotions under control.

2. Be supportive and reassuring to your child.

3. If you believe your child may have suffered pain, physical injury, or penetration, take him to the doctor or emergency room.

4. Call the police. Be prepared to explain why you think your child has been molested and whom you suspect.

5. Obtain therapy by a trained professional for your child and your family.

WHAT TO DO IF YOUR CHILD IS MISSING

EMERGENCY CHECKLIST:

1. Call the police. Be prepared to give a physical description of your child and the clothes he was wearing, his last known whereabouts, and a recent photograph.

2. Cooperate with the police to get yourself cleared as a suspect as quickly as possible so that search efforts can be properly directed. Establish a relationship of trust and cooperation with the police and let them do their job.

3. Call local news media and provide appropriate information and photographs. Establish and maintain a partnership with news media to promote ongoing publicity about your missing child.

4. Call the NCMEC (1-800-THE-LOST) and provide all relevant information, photographs, etc.

5. Call the Jimmy Ryce Center (1-800-JIM-RYCE) for assistance.

6. Arrange for someone to monitor your home telephone at all times.

7. Organize your friends, relatives, colleagues, and neighbors to help with the search.

8. Use your contacts and friends-of-friends to get assistance in your search and publicity efforts.

9. Prepare flyers and posters with your child's picture and relevant information. Distribute these to police, the news media, and throughout the community—to stores and restaurants, shopping malls, public buildings, gas stations, schools, everywhere you can think of.

10. Consider offering a reward for information about your child. Contact an attorney to help you with the details.

RESOURCES

The National Center for Missing and Exploited Children
Arlington, Virginia
Toll-free hotline   1-800-THE-LOST
Manager of Legislative Affairs   (703) 235-3900

The National Center for Missing and Exploited Children
Florida Branch
Director Nancy McBride   (561) 848-1900

The National Center for Missing and Exploited Children
California Branch
Director Kathy DePeri   (714) 508-0150

The National Center for Missing and Exploited Children
South Carolina Branch
Director Margaret Frierson   (803) 750-7055

The National Center for Missing and Exploited Children
New York Branch
Director Gay-LeClerc Qader   (716) 242-0900

Among the many valuable services the NCMEC provides are:

• A twenty-four-hour toll-free hotline for parents to report missing children, 1-800-THE-LOST (1 800 843-5678)

• Missing Child Alert—instant exposure by computer or public service announcements in breaking cases, distributed via satellite across the country

• Dissemination of information on missing children nationwide to law enforcement, the news media, and the public by fax and computers, and in multimedia kiosks in high-traffic areas such as airports

• Access to the FBI's National Crime Information Center data banks for missing persons, wanted persons, and unidentified persons

• Maintenance of a computer data bank to track leads, identify patterns among cases, and tie cases together

• "KIDS AND COMPANY: Together for Safety"—a safety education program for children in kindergarten through sixth grade

• Booklets, publications, and educational materials available free by calling the hotline at 1-800-THE-LOST

Carol Cope is a Miami-based attorney, psychologist, mother, and writer. She is the author of the critically acclaimed and bestselling *In the Fast Lane: A True Story of Murder in Miami* (Simon & Schuster, 1993).